Preparing safety reports:

Control of Major Accident Hazards Regulations 1999

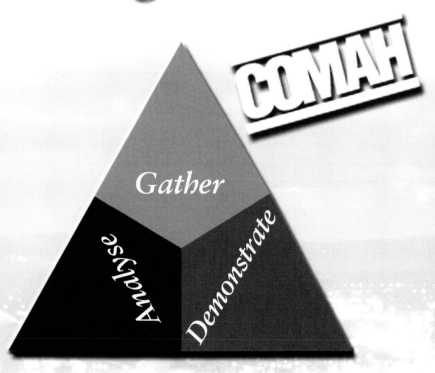

Gather

Analyse

Demonstrate

COMAH

HSG190

HSE BOOKS

Contents

The Control of Major Accident Hazards Regulations 1999 (COMAH) implement the Seveso II Directive, and are important for controlling major accident hazards involving dangerous substances, in Great Britain. The Regulations are enforced by HSE and the respective Environment Agency acting as a competent authority. It is for this reason that this guidance is a joint publication.

A COMAH safety report is an important part of these controls for those sites with the greatest hazards. It is a concise description of safe and environmentally sound operation during the life cycle of facilities processing or storing dangerous substances. The information gathered for the safety report should identify major accidents, describe the measures in place for preventing such accidents and limiting the consequences of any which do occur. The safety report is evidence that an operator has carefully scrutinised these preventive and control measures.

This book is a practical guide for those who have to write safety reports. It explains that the safety report should contain information about your operation in enough detail to demonstrate that there are adequate safety measures to prevent major accidents to people or the environment, and to limit the consequences of any major accidents that may occur.

Preparing a safety report takes time, so work out a plan and start early. If you have prepared a safety report before under the Control of Industrial Major Hazards Regulations 1984 (CIMAH), you will find there are differences in the new requirements. For instance, there is an increased emphasis on providing information on environmental matters and the demonstration of measures, particularly the management arrangements, for preventing and limiting major accidents to the environment, as well as to people. However, much of the information required in a safety report remains the same. This book will help you identify the issues you should consider.

In all the detail, do not lose sight of the goal of preparing a safety report which is to clearly demonstrate that your facilities are, and will continue to be, run safely with regard to the protection of people and the environment.

We commend this guidance to you.

Signed:

Jenny Bacon
(Director General, HSE)

Ed Gallagher
(Chief Executive,
Environment Agency)

Alasdair C Paton
(Chief Executive,
(Scottish Environment
Protection Agency)

Introduction

Who is this book for?

1   If you are operating a COMAH site and are required to write a safety report, this book is for you.

2   COMAH is short for the Control of Major Accident Hazards Regulations 1999, which came into force on 1 April 1999. The Regulations apply to operators with specified quantities of defined dangerous substances on their site, and require the operators to take all measures necessary to prevent major accidents. There are two thresholds for dangerous substances held on any particular establishment. For establishments with quantities above the higher threshold, COMAH places more duties on the operator, including a requirement to prepare a safety report on which the competent authority for COMAH must give its conclusions to the operator. Details on the application and the full requirements of COMAH are discussed in the HSE guide to the Regulations.[1]

3   References to 'accidents' or 'safety' throughout the book apply equally to risks to people and to the environment. Thus, health and safety issues become safety, health and environmental concerns.

4   The competent authority which enforces COMAH is the Health and Safety Executive (HSE) and the Environment Agency in England and Wales, and HSE and the Scottish Environment Protection Agency in Scotland. As a reference, this book will refer to the 'competent authority' throughout the text.

What does this book do?

5   This book gives comprehensive guidance on how to write a COMAH safety report. It is not intended to be a legal commentary but a practical guide, and is structured in the order that you are likely to write your safety report. It uses the competent authority's assessment criteria as the basis of the guidance. These criteria will be used by the competent authority to come to conclusions about your safety report.

6   An HSE document *Safety report assessment manual* contains the assessment criteria and how they should be used by the competent authority, the principles on which the competent authority's assessment process is founded, the procedures themselves and many other of the competent authority's internal procedures relating to safety reports. This document can be read by visiting the public registers held in the local offices of the agencies (see glossary), where a copy is kept in each office. It can also be read by accessing the Chemical and Hazardous Installations Division (CHID) page of the HSE site on the world wide web. The address is http://www.open.gov.uk/hse/chid/index.htm.

What does it cover?

7   This book is structured to set out the main issues involved in writing a safety report. These are outlined in Chapter 1, along with information about when a safety report is required.

8   Chapter 2 outlines the required contents of a safety report and the format of the remainder of this book. Chapters 3-7 describe in detail the type of information that should be included in a safety report. This is based on the minimum information required by Schedule 4 Part 2 of COMAH. Guidance on the extent of the information required is based on:

(a)   HSE's experience as the competent authority for assessing CIMAH safety reports; and

(b)   the views of the competent authority as to what is required under COMAH to meet the purposes of safety reports detailed in Schedule 4 Part 1.

9   You, as a report writer, can decide to present the information in any way you wish, however the chapters in this book are ordered in a way which the competent authority thinks is logical to make the necessary demonstrations. Reports presented in this way should also be quicker and easier for the competent authority to assess.

10   The suggested format means that you present:

(a)   site information common to all parts (guidance is in Chapter 3);

(b) information on the management arrangements and safety management systems (Chapter 4);

(c) information about individual installations and processes, identification of major accident scenarios, assessment of their consequences and/or risk analysis (Chapter 5);

(d) information about the measures to prevent or limit the consequences of a major accident (Chapter 6); and

(e) information about emergency response (Chapter 7).

11 There can be mixing of these to suit your circumstances, such as multi-installation sites where you may wish to put as much common information as possible in a 'core' report to avoid repetition. For example, you could refer to generic major accident scenarios or consequence assessments for more than one installation or part of an installation.

12 The nature and extent of the information needed in a safety report depends on the size and complexity of your establishment, the major accident hazards involved, the nature of the environment around the site and the type and purpose of the report. Some safety reports will need to include a full range of information, while others will not. The following examples illustrate the extent of information that may be needed:

(a) *Existing establishments*
The full range of information is likely to be required in a safety report for an existing establishment. An existing establishment* (see glossary) is one that was operational on the day that COMAH came into force and contained at least the lower of the two threshold quantities of dangerous substances.

(b) *New establishments*
Reports for new establishments - ones which are built on 'green field land' and which started operating after COMAH came into force - will usually be prepared in two stages:

(i) before starting construction of the first installation on site; and

(ii) before dangerous substances are put into the installation.

At a new site, there is an opportunity to get safety right at the design stage. For example, information should be focused on hazard identification, consequence assessment and justifying design options to prevent a major accident. For more details on arrangements for dealing with new sites see paragraphs 80-87. You should also discuss your timetable with the local office of HSE or the appropriate Environment Agency.

(c) *Changes to establishments*
Amendments to reports are required where changes are planned to an existing establishment. They are also required after a review, which you are legally required to undertake if you decide there are significant safety implications. The focus of information in this variation of a safety report depends on what the changes are, for example changes to the installation or to the management systems.

How do I start?

13 We recommend that you browse through the whole book and then plan your safety report, preferably following the order of the chapters, before drafting the detail based on this guidance.

14 It is vital that you start with a clear understanding of why you are writing the safety report. To help you gain this, see Chapter 1.

15 This book gives a great deal of detail about what should be included in a safety report. Chapter 2 should help you understand the principles of what you are trying to achieve and gives a suggested structure to follow. A structured approach makes writing the safety report easier. It also makes the assessment easier for the competent authority.

* The COMAH Regulations use the term 'establishment' to mean the whole site.

16   You should also understand what the legal requirements are, concerning the information to be provided in a safety report. These are given in Appendix 1. The Appendix cross-refers to the guidance provided throughout the book.

Links with other COMAH guidance

17   This book only deals with writing a COMAH safety report. Further guidance is being produced on other parts of the COMAH Regulations.[1-6] The starting point is the guide to the COMAH Regulations,[1] which reproduces the Regulations and also gives guidance on what the Regulations mean. This book supports that guidance and gives practical help in writing safety reports.

18   Guidance is also being prepared on the interpretation of a major accident to the environment for the purposes of the COMAH Regulations[3] and on environmental risk assessment as regards COMAH.[4]

Exceptions

19   You must provide information about all the dangerous substances on your site and the major accident scenarios. You are entitled to limit the information you provide in the safety report about a particular dangerous substance if you believe it cannot give rise to a major accident. You should however apply to the competent authority for a decision to allow you to do this. The guide to the COMAH Regulations[1] at regulation 7 (12) provides information to help you.

Chapter 1

Safety reports - purpose and background information

Introduction and purpose of safety reports

Introduction

20   This chapter is the first step in preparing your safety report. It will give you a good understanding of what a safety report is, when it is required, and what information to include in it. Some key terminology is identified and explained, and there are guidelines for general presentation.

Overall purpose

21   A safety report makes a positive contribution to the prevention of major accidents on your site, and to the limitation of their consequences to people and the environment.

22   Firstly, it is a document in which you present information in a way that shows you have measures in place to prevent major accidents and limit their consequences. It can only be successful in this aim if you have systematically examined your site activities, the potential for major accidents, and listed what you have done or are going do to prevent major accidents.

23   Secondly, the safety report is a demonstration that the safety measures on site have been arrived at as a result of a systematic process. The value in writing a safety report is that it shows that you have investigated your safety measures, whether organisational, technical or in terms of how people contribute to safety on your site. It also shows that you have arrangements in place to put right any shortcomings you identify.

24   In this way, writing the safety report shows how you meet the fundamental duty of COMAH - the prevention and limitation of major accidents.

What are the main differences between CIMAH and COMAH safety reports?

25   There are substantial differences in emphasis between the two types of safety report, and significant differences in the content. CIMAH safety reports were mainly focused on providing information. In other words, they were required to give a description of *what* measures were in place. COMAH safety reports will provide much of the same information, but must clearly demonstrate that measures are in place to prevent major accidents and limit the consequences if they occur. In other words, they should describe not only *what*, but *why* these particular measures together are thought to prevent and limit major accidents.

26   Much greater emphasis is also placed on measures to protect the environment.

27   Appendix 2 gives more details about the differences between CIMAH and COMAH reports.

To whom should you submit the safety report?

28   The safety report should be submitted to your local HSE office, who will receive and acknowledge the report on behalf of the competent authority. HSE and the agencies will work together under these Regulations to assess the safety reports they receive.

Timescales for safety reports

When is a safety report required?

29   A safety report is required if the quantity of a defined dangerous substance present on your establishment equals or exceeds the quantity given in COMAH (for details look at Parts 2 and 3 of Schedule 3 at Column 1). Included in the calculations are dangerous substances which you anticipate to be present, and those which you reasonably believe may be produced during a loss of control of an industrial chemical process, for example during an uncontrolled or runaway reaction.

30   A substance comes within the definition of a dangerous substance if it:

(a)   is named in Part 2 of Schedule 1 of COMAH, such as chlorine; or

(b) has properties which classify it as 'very toxic', 'toxic', 'oxidising', 'explosive', 'flammable', 'highly flammable', 'extremely flammable', 'violent reactions with water' or 'dangerous to the environment', as classified by the Chemicals (Hazard Information and Packaging for Supply) Regulations 1994[7] (CHIP). These have been amended by 1996, 1997, 1998 and 1999 Amendment Regulations, and you need to check annually that you are up to date with these Regulations.

31 The quantities of each type of dangerous substance determine whether a safety report is required. The quantities vary enormously. For example, a safety report is required for as little as 20 tonnes of a 'very toxic' substance, or in the case of a 'flammable' substance, 50 000 tonnes.

32 Full details of the qualifying quantities are in the guide to the COMAH Regulations.[1] The guide also gives details of the rules for aggregating different substances together, which must be carried out to determine if a safety report is required.

The timing of your safety report

33 If you have sent a CIMAH safety report to HSE, your COMAH report will be due according to the table in Appendix 3. This appendix summarises the requirements for initial safety reports for existing establishments, ie those that were subject to COMAH on 1 April 1999. Reports for new establishments, and for revisions after reviews, are dealt with later in this chapter.

34 If you did not submit a CIMAH report but are required to do so under COMAH, then the safety report must be submitted by 3 February 2002.

35 You need to identify the correct date so that you can plan the work and submit your completed safety report on time. COMAH allows you sufficient time to prepare your report. However in the case of the first deadline date of February 2000, if you believe you have exceptional reasons for not being able to meet this deadline, you should contact the competent authority and explain your

reasons. The competent authority may extend this first deadline date if it is satisfied that there are exceptional circumstances and you could not have planned to do the work in time.

> **Describing the information that has to be included in a safety report, and how it has to be presented**

What information is required in the safety report?

36 The COMAH Regulations detail what has to be in the safety report. It must contain the information set out in Schedule 4 Part 2 which is sufficient for the purposes set out in COMAH.

The purposes of a safety report as set out in Schedule 4 Part 1

37 The purposes are that the safety report should make a series of **demonstrations**. These are that:

(a) a major accident prevention policy (MAPP) and a safety management system (SMS) for implementing it have been put into effect;

(b) major accident hazards have been identified;

(c) the measures necessary have been taken to prevent major accidents and to limit their consequences for people and the environment;

(d) adequate safety and reliability have been incorporated into the design, construction, operation and maintenance of any installation linked to major accident hazards within the establishment. This also applies to any equipment and infrastructure connected with the installation's operation; and

(e) an on-site emergency plan has been drawn up.

38 Certain information is also required to meet the purposes of a safety report under Schedule 4 Part 1. These are:

(a) supplying information to enable the off-site emergency plan to be drawn up; and

(b) providing sufficient information to the competent authority to enable it to provide advice to planning authorities about the siting of new activities or developments around existing establishments.

Information required as set out in Schedule 4 Part 2

39   This part describes the minimum information that should be included in a safety report to meet the purposes. The information should relate to:

(a) the management system and the organisation of the establishment with a view to major accident prevention;

(b) description of the environment of the establishment;

(c) description of the installation;

(d) hazard identification, consequence assessment, risk analysis and prevention methods; and

(e) measures of prevention and intervention to limit the consequences of a major accident.

40   What this means is you should:

(a) concentrate on providing information, using matters listed in Schedule 4 Part 2, that relate to major accident hazards from the dangerous substances on site, as the framework for what is required;

(b) analyse the information and present it in a way that makes the demonstrations required by Schedule 4 Part 1; and

(c) give enough information to enable others to draw up the off-site emergency plan, and to enable the competent authority to provide advice to planning authorities about the siting of new activities or developments around your site.

41   In short, you need to provide enough information and present it in such a way that the competent authority can see that you have made the required demonstrations.

42   You may have already provided some of this information for other purposes. For example, suitable descriptions of some of the installations may have formed part of an earlier Integrated Pollution Control (IPC) application. Alternatively a site plan with inventories may have been submitted to the local hazardous substances authority for hazardous substance consent which HSE receives as a statutory consultee. In such cases, you are not required to prepare this information again so long as it is suitable for the purpose and sufficient. However the information should be cross-referenced in your report and confirmed as being still relevant and correct. Even so it is strongly recommended that you copy this information as part of your safety report submission, to help speed the assessment and avoid confusion.

43   Appendix 1 illustrates how the purposes - the demonstrations and the minimum information requirements - are related.

What does 'demonstration' mean?

44   This is the key to understanding the purposes of a safety report.

45   To make a 'demonstration' means to show, justify or make the case/argument through the information given. Initially, the competent authority will take at face value any statements you make in the safety report and presume they are true, unless it has information to the contrary. However, inspectors may ask to see paperwork to prove your claims, particularly as part of an inspection programme based on the information in your safety report.

46   Making a demonstration does not mean 'proving beyond reasonable doubt'. So for example, if a safety report states that a vessel is manufactured to a particular European Standard, there is no need to include copies of certificates which prove that it is built to that standard. It is enough to quote the standard

and say why it is appropriate for the vessel concerned (eg by comparing key design parameters, such as pressure and temperature limits, with the scope of the standard). Where commonly found standards are referred to for a number of vessels, then a general comment outlining their general application is sufficient. If you have not made conventional use of a standard in some part of the design but have adopted some other approach which you consider appropriate, you should explain why.

47   Most standards have a restricted scope of application such as restrictions to certain materials of construction or certain operating conditions (temperature or pressure limits). For example, ASME VIII Div 1, for pressure vessels only, allows the use of code material but since this is not available in Europe, the use of equivalent material is the norm. Whereas the use of BS 2654 (non-refrigerated atmospheric storage tanks) at temperatures or pressures outside its scope could require rigorous justification.

48   The safety report should justify the use of a standard which is out of date or withdrawn, particularly if the report relates to the design of new plant.

49   You may have relatively old plant, which complies with out-of-date standards, or even incomplete records for justifying design decisions. In these cases, you should still be able to show that the design is fit for purpose. However, you should also show that you have established additional arrangements, where appropriate, to prevent or limit a major accident, such as more frequent testing or examination regimes for plant and equipment, or more reliance on operator control. These arrangements should be described, including, in the case of operator controls, whether there has been increased emphasis on training and monitoring of performance. The competent authority may well focus on human factor issues in these cases.

50   In summary, the safety report should demonstrate why you think the necessary measures are needed to prevent or limit a major accident. Subsequent inspections by the competent authority will examine these measures in more detail, and show whether the measures are being taken and are effective.

51   COMAH applies to a wide range of establishments, differing in size, number of employees, complexity, resources and expertise, technology, culture, and the environment surrounding the site. All sites have one thing in common: the potential for a major accident, albeit covering different hazards. It would be unreasonable for the safety report for a small ammonium nitrate store to be similar to a report for a major oil refinery, but both must make the same demonstrations.

52   The same quality of demonstration has to be made whether the establishment is large or small, whether the operator is a multi-national company or a small business employing few people. Sufficient information has to be available to make the link between the major accident scenarios and the measures in place. The amount of information provided in the safety report, and the way it is presented, can however be different.

53   The following examples illustrate this point.

Example 1

54   A majority of operators run well-known and straightforward manufacturing processes or storage sites. This means these operators can rely heavily on published guidance or standards to justify the measures they use, as long as they show they understand the limits of application of those standards or guidance.

55   Many operators have simple management structures, particularly the smaller sites, and the management arrangements can be described briefly. The organisations are compact, the arrangements for control are direct, and the need for demonstrating good communications may be minimal because communication is not likely to be such a significant an issue as in a large organisation.

56   For example, the LP Gas Association guidance on liquefied petroleum gas (LPG) storage and the HSE guidance on the storage of flammable liquids (HSG176) provide much useful information on what is good industry practice. Such guidance can be used in support of your demonstration. If you use the

information about separation distances, then you should understand their purpose and appreciate their limits. These separation distances are not given to protect people from the consequences of a loss of containment from the tank, but to prevent an incident beyond the separation distance from affecting the tank. Additional risk assessment is required to consider off-site risks which follow the principles in Chapter 5 and Appendix 4. Further, this guidance is basically restricted to storage and does not cover process plant, where there could be different requirements, such as for fire protection, separation distances and methods of isolation.

Example 2

57   Sites with large numbers of employees and complex installations are likely to have more detailed management structures. A description of these structures with the relevant roles and responsibilities and, for example, the demonstration of good communication between those with responsibilities, play a very important part in this type of safety report. If processes are complex or unusual, then more information should be included, explaining how the operator has selected appropriate measures for the major accident scenarios. The contribution of these measures to the overall risk control also needs to be explained.

58   The risk assessment demonstrations will be more complicated than in Example 1. For straightforward processes included in the large site's activities, the use of published guidance and standards for demonstrations can be the same as for Example 1 in many cases.

Example 3

59   A safety report may describe a flammable gases vent system linked to a flare stack which is common to a number of vessels throughout the establishment. This is a critical item of plant for ensuring containment, and the safety report will need to describe its design parameters. The safety report should describe how the system is designed to prevent deflagration and detonation spreading

to other plants and installations, for example by the use of flame arrestors, and describe what the chances are of loss of containment and major accident. The safety report should mention that the operator has identified an appropriate flame arrestor for the different types of flammable gas, all properly identified, that are likely to be present.

60   In these circumstances, there is no need to include details of the make and model of the flame arrestor or include manufacturers' catalogues with detailed specifications. The information provided will show sufficient description as to why the design is adequate. Further investigation or verification might be carried out by the competent authority as part of any subsequent inspection, to check the adequacy of the design and the management systems relating to procurement and construction.

Example 4

61   A safety report describes the bunding arrangements for tanks with very toxic chemicals, which could cause harm to the environment if released. As this is a critical measure for limiting loss of containment, the safety report should describe its design parameters. The report should also describe the filling and emptying operations, and the systems to prevent a major accidental release including procedures and design such as the use and location of isolation valves. The competent authority may then carry out a more detailed examination of these features as part of its inspection programme.

Discussion

62   What the four examples illustrate is that the amount of information you have to provide and the depth of your demonstration depend on a number of factors:

(a)   the size and complexity of the establishment, for example it normally takes more effort to describe an oil refinery than a warehouse;

(b)   the potential to cause harm, for example the operator of a warehouse storing many different chemicals may need to supply more information about potential consequences than the operator of an LPG storage facility. (Both have to describe the worst case scenario (see glossary) and a range of scenarios relating to the classes of chemicals stored as well as giving a description of the likelihood of the events);

(c) the extent of hazard analysis and risk assessment that you have to undertake, for example it is very likely you will have to undertake a hazard and operability study (HAZOP) and a detailed consequence analysis if you have:

    (i) innovative processes;

    (ii) processes and activities where there are no recognised standards or benchmarks;

    (iii) complex hazards; or

    (iv) substantial potential for loss of life or severe damage to the environment beyond the immediate vicinity of the site.

In some cases, a quantified risk assessment will help to analyse the risks and if clearly presented, including the important assumptions, will help justify the necessary measures to take; and

(d) the extent to which you can demonstrate safety using the following approaches:

    (i) competent authority guidance - this is issued jointly or separately by HSE and the relevant Agency;

    (ii) industry standards - with these, and the competent authority's guidance, the scope of the guidance and its limitations have to be understood and related to the risks from the major accident hazards;

    (iii) manufacturers' standards or advice and internal company standards - these are not sufficient on their own without a full description of the

underlying rationale, including where they deviate from published standards;

    (iv) expert advice, including consultants - this can be a very good source of information for demonstrating and justifying measures, particularly through risk assessment. However, the source data needs to based on real on-site conditions; and

    (v) experience - this is unlikely to be comprehensive because it is based on an individual's personal experience or single-site experience, though it may offer important evidence on specific issues.

63   Where an operator opts to demonstrate that additional measures are not necessary, such arguments need only show this 'on balance'. The operator need not prove it 'beyond reasonable doubt'.

Role of a safety report in the continuing operation of the site

Is the safety report a 'licence to operate'?

64   The safety report is not part of a licence to operate. The conclusions given by the competent authority should not be seen as a permission for continued operation. The report provides information about the measures to prevent or limit the consequences of a major accident. If these measures are seriously deficient, the competent authority will prohibit operation.

65   A safety report only needs to make its demonstrations and describe the measures used to control the major accident hazards, at the time it is written. It is not meant to be an operational blueprint. Nevertheless, it should reflect accurately what goes on. If there is a change after the safety report is written, which could have significant repercussions for the prevention and mitigation of major accidents, you should review the report and submit the details of the revision to the competent authority (see the guide to the COMAH Regulations[1]).

What happens to the safety report?

66   The report will be placed on a public register unless you advise the competent authority in writing at the time of submission that certain information should not be disclosed in this way. Advice on what to do in such a case is given in paragraph 77.

67   The competent authority will read the report to:

(a)   examine the information to see whether it is sufficient;

(b)   assess whether the purposes have been achieved, ie whether the required demonstrations have been made; and

form its conclusions in doing (a) and (b).

68   The report will be used by the competent authority to:

(a)   prompt prohibition action where certain measures appear to be seriously deficient in preventing a major accident or limiting the consequences of one (and this is confirmed by a site visit); and

(b)   decide which installations, parts of installations or activities at your establishment should be included in the competent authority's inspection programme.

69   This process is all part of the assessment of the safety report by the competent authority. Assessment by the competent authority will require:

(a)   an Assessment Manager (AM) and a plan for each safety report being assessed; and

(b)   a team of competent assessors drawn from both HSE and the environment agencies.

70   You will be given the name of the AM for each report that you submit when the competent authority acknowledges receipt of your report. The AM will be your normal contact for matters concerning your report.

71   Members of the assessment team will examine the information in the safety report and assess whether it meets the purposes required by Schedule 4 of COMAH, by reviewing the report against assessment criteria. You may be asked for further information during the assessment process if the team consider there is insufficient information.

Conclusions about the report from the competent authority

72   The assessment team will come to conclusions on the safety report, using their professional judgement.

73   The conclusions will be based on:

(a)   whether any serious deficiencies are identified. If so, the competent authority will take immediate action. Prohibition action is only taken if the serious deficiencies are confirmed by a site visit; and

(b)   whether the report (and any additional information obtained during the assessment process) is sufficient to meet the purposes (ie whether the demonstrations have been made).

74   If the demonstrations have not been made within the report, then the assessment team will decide what they need from you. Normally, the AM will ask you to send further information, but if the report falls so far short of meeting its purpose, the report may be returned to you and a re-submission required.

75   The competent authority will send a conclusions letter to you, outlining the points described in the previous paragraphs, and advising on what issues they may wish to follow up in subsequent inspections. The assessment team may wish to present their findings to you at a meeting.

76   The competent authority aims to send its conclusions to you on your safety report (and its five-yearly revision) within 12 months of receipt, unless there are serious delays in providing further information requested by the

competent authority. Where a report is submitted because modifications have meant a variation to the report, the competent authority will send its conclusions within six months of receipt. The arrangements concerning new sites are a little different and you should refer to paragraphs 84 and 87 for further information on timescales.

Are safety reports publicly available?

77   The competent authority will maintain a register of COMAH information available to the public. This register will include a copy of your safety report and the conclusions of the competent authority assessment team about the report. Information can be excluded from the register if it is either commercially confidential, personally confidential or contrary to the interests of national security. If you intend to apply for exclusion of information from the register on these grounds, it may help to discuss it with your AM beforehand:

(a)   Commercial or personal confidentiality
If you believe there is information in your report that should be excluded from the register on the grounds of commercial or personal confidentiality, you should apply for its exclusion to the competent authority when you submit your report. For new installations which require a safety report in two stages, if you chose to submit your report in parts at the pre-construction stage, you should make any confidentiality applications when you submit the final part of the pre-construction stage.

Before the competent authority's conclusions are placed on the public register, it will send you a copy and ask whether any information should be excluded on the grounds of commercial or personal confidentiality, or national security. Your application for confidentiality should contain sufficient detail to enable the competent authority to adequately consider your case. These applications will be determined within 28 days of receipt. If you are not satisfied with the outcome you may appeal to the Secretary of State. Your local HSE/Agency office can advise where to lodge an appeal.

(b)   National security
The Secretary of State may write general directions, which will secure the exclusion of certain information from the register (at the time of printing - July 1999 - there were no such directions). If you believe there is information in your report, or in the conclusions on it, which should be excluded from the register because it is contrary to the interests of national security, you should contact your local office of HSE, who will advise you where to write to. These applications must be made when you submit your report, or in the case of the conclusions, when you receive them from the competent authority.

78   No information will be placed on the register until all issues of confidentiality and national security have been determined.

79   The registers will be maintained at local agency offices and reviewed on a five-yearly basis.

> ### Additional information for new sites and multi-installation sites

New establishments

80   As explained in the introduction, different arrangements for preparing safety reports must be followed for establishments which are new to COMAH.

81   You are required to submit the part of the safety report relating to design and construction to the competent authority before the start of construction, with the balance of information supplied before operation starts. The start of the operation is considered to be the time when dangerous substances are introduced for the first time, even if this is at the commissioning stage.

82   At the stage before construction, you are allowed to send information to the competent authority as a series of documents submitted at different times (a 'rolling' submission). This enables you to provide the necessary information at the appropriate stage in the design and development of a particular project. You need to be in close dialogue with

the competent authority during this stage, so that the AM understands and agrees to the arrangements and can plan as quick a response as possible. This ensures that you can proceed with confidence through each stage of the project. For each document submitted, the competent authority will only expect the level of detail that is appropriate to the stage of development of the design.

83   At the stage before construction, the information required in the safety report includes:

(a)   a description of the site and its surroundings, and the dangerous substances to be used, all of which are discussed in Chapter 3;

(b)   the management systems used to ensure the appropriate design and to be followed to ensure the plant is constructed to its design intent, as discussed in Chapter 4;

(c)   the major accident scenarios described in Chapter 5;

(d)   conceptual design issues, such as the selection of process options and plant layout;

(e)   more detailed design issues such as materials of construction and secondary containment, as the project develops;

and the principles of (d) and (e) are discussed in Chapter 6.

84   You will not be able to proceed to the construction phase of the project until the competent authority has given its conclusions on this information. If you have made a 'rolling' submission then the competent authority should be able to complete this stage quickly. However, with little prior information, this stage may take up to three months.

85   The remaining information required by COMAH to meet the purposes of a safety report should be submitted before any dangerous substances are introduced to the plant. Information will need to be completed on, for example, management arrangements, operational controls and emergency plans,

which it was not reasonable to provide during the pre-construction phase. The competent authority will also require information about any changes made to the design and construction since the pre-construction submission.

86   The two parts of the report (ie the parts submitted before construction and operation) should allow the competent authority to see the whole argument on how the measures taken to prevent major accidents or limit their consequences, have been arrived at.

87   Operation cannot begin until the competent authority has given its conclusions on the remaining information you have provided, and assessed the information provided as a whole package. This may take the competent authority up to six months after receiving all the information. This could be less if the pre-construction submission was comprehensive, or if you also had substantial discussion with the competent authority during the second stage.

Multi-installation sites

88   Under CIMAH, safety reports were prepared for individual industrial activities and installations, which resulted in a number of safety reports being prepared for some sites. COMAH requires a report for the site, but allows operators to continue with their practice of preparing reports for individual installations. COMAH therefore allows the safety report for the establishment to be submitted in parts. Normally, common site-wide features, such as an overview of the site, site management arrangements, surrounding environment and information about site emergency plans can be included in a 'core' report to avoid duplicating information in each 'part report'. However, the individual installation reports cannot be assessed by the competent authority without the information provided in the core report.

89   The timetable for submission of these 'part reports' for installations follows the rules tabled in Appendix 3. The competent authority is required to inform you of its conclusions for each 'part report' and on completion of the full report after all the parts have been submitted. To ensure that you have

provided all the information and made the necessary demonstrations under Schedule 4 for the whole site, you should review the information supplied after all the 'part reports' have been submitted.

Reviewing and revising safety reports

90   COMAH requires you to review your safety report and keep it up to date by revising it. A review is required:

(a)   if there are new facts or there is new technical knowledge about safety matters;

(b)   when you propose to modify the site, an installation on site, any process, or the nature and quantity of a dangerous substance, if you think any of these could have significant repercussions for the prevention of major accidents or limiting their consequences;

(c)   whenever you make a change to the SMS, which could have significant repercussions for the prevention of major accidents or limiting their consequences;

(d)   at least every five years.

The competent authority will also require it, if the report has not been reviewed for the reasons outlined in (a) - (d) above. The following paragraphs explain these requirements in more detail.

(a) New facts or new technical knowledge

91   You are required to review your safety report and, if necessary, revise it to take account of new facts or new technical knowledge about safety issues. The following examples illustrate the type of event that would trigger a review:

(a)   new knowledge about the nature of a substance handled, such as a change in classification;

(b)   new knowledge and developments in technical or procedural controls;

(c)   changes in the principles of control, for example it may not always be possible to maintain plant in 'as built' condition; or

(d)   changes to the environment outside the site which may alter the risks off-site from a major accident.

92   You should review and, if you conclude it is necessary, revise the safety report as soon as possible after the new knowledge or facts become known.

93   The competent authority would prefer the updated report to be submitted as a whole, with the changes clearly marked. However, if your original report was submitted in loose-leaf ring binders, it is acceptable to send just the amended pages with the changes clearly marked.

(b) & (c) Modifications

94   The report must be revised in the event of any changes which could have significant repercussions with respect to the prevention or limitation of major accidents. An explanation of what is meant by 'significant repercussions' can be found in the guide to the Regulations.[1]

95   You should consider whether changes to your safety management systems might have significant repercussions on your ability to prevent or limit the consequences of a major accident. Examples of the types of changes which are likely to be significant include:

(a)   proposals for significant reorganisation of the management structure, or changes to the MAPP or safety management system;

(b)   proposals involving delayering or reducing staff, to a significant extent;

(c)   a decision to adopt multi-skilling in relation to the operation or maintenance of the establishment;

(d)   proposals to significantly increase the amount of contracting; and

(e)   a takeover or other significant change to the overall management of the organisation.

96   You must review and, if necessary, revise your report before these changes are made. You should discuss with the competent authority whether you are going to: amend and resubmit the whole report (in which case the changes should be clearly marked); submit only the pages which have changed; or submit a separate stand-alone document describing and justifying the changes, which will then form part of the safety report.

97   Usually, the last option has the advantage of being easier to prepare and examine because it focuses all the information and arguments together. This report can then be edited into the main text of the safety report later. A convenient time would be when the five-yearly review and any update is required.

98   The new information provided in a revised report and the required demonstrations should be to the same extent and quality as for other variations of safety reports, but focused on the proposed changes which have led to the report being prepared.

(d) Five-yearly review

99   In addition to the required reviews mentioned previously, you are required, in any event, to review your safety report every five years. You do not need to revise it unless there are changes to be made, but after a period of five years, it is likely that you will need to. If you don't, you must still notify the competent authority that changes were not considered necessary.

100   As part of the five-year review you should examine any small changes over the five years that were not considered significant to justify a revision at the time, but which will have had a cumulative effect over the five years.

101   Operators who submitted their safety report in parts must review each part not later than five years after it was submitted. However, the review of the final part has to consider whether all the parts together fulfil the purposes set out in Schedule 4 Part 1 and contain all the information detailed in Schedule 4 Part 2.

102   This review of the whole report, at the time you review the final part, is to ensure that the whole report fully covers the infrastructure and all the inter-related on-site measures which might have an effect on the causes or consequences of major accidents.

Required by the competent authority whenever the circumstances in (a) - (d) apply

103   The competent authority may require you to prepare a report if an inspector believes that there have been changes to the information described which have not been identified by you or have been ignored. The reasons for this will be discussed with you before the request is formally made.

Structuring and presenting the information in a safety report

104   Chapter 1 provides guidance on the steps you should take to compile a safety report. This chapter outlines a structure which you can follow in preparing a safety report, by explaining the purpose in providing the detailed information described in Chapters 3-7. It also advises on how to start your preparation for writing a safety report, and how to use and present the information. Each of the following chapters gives detailed information about what should be included.

105   To help you to relate the advice in the text to the legal requirements, Appendix 1 lists the information that is required by Schedule 4 of COMAH, and indicates where in this book you can find guidance for each requirement. Some requirements are repeated in more than one chapter because the information can be used for different purposes.

Summary of Chapters 3-7, by explaining the purpose and giving an outline of the required information

Description of establishment and the management arrangements

106   Chapter 3 describes the extent of the information required to allow the competent authority to have a clear overview of the establishment, its purpose, location, activities and intrinsic hazards, services and technical equipment for preventing and controlling major accidents. For multi-installation sites, this information is often included as part of the core information common to the whole establishment. More detailed information, such as a description of safety-related control equipment, can be covered in the description of individual installations.

107   As the organisational aspects are a fundamental part of your safety system, these are best described early on in your safety report. A suggested framework of what the competent authority expects to find is described in Chapter 4, but the competent authority will be looking for robust arrangements to show how you arrive at the necessary measures to prevent or control major accidents. The measures that you

provide and subsequently describe in the safety report will also demonstrate whether you have put into effect the management arrangements you describe. For multi-installation sites, differences in arrangements can be identified and described in the part of the report dealing with a particular installation.

Measures to prevent or limit the consequences of major accident

108   Chapters 5, 6 and 7 aim to describe how to make the link between the hazards identified on site and the measures you believe are necessary to prevent a major accident or limit the consequences of such an accident.

109   There is a flow of related information required, covering the main activities on site and the processes that go on. This flow is discussed in the following sequence:

Chapter 5
    Initiating agent, ie primary causes
    Consequence assessment

Chapter 6
    Measures provided to:
    - avoid (inherent safety approach)
    - prevent (prevent initiation)
    - control (prevent escalation)

Chapter 7
    Measures provided to:
    - limit (emergency measures)

The measures can be engineering measures, systems and procedural or human factors such as training. Most likely they will be a combination of each.

110   Your findings and conclusions from the risk analyses should summarise the relationship between the hazards and risks. They should also demonstrate that you have taken the necessary measures to prevent and limit the consequences of major accidents, and that there is adequate safety and reliability of the installation, equipment and infrastructure during their lifetime.

111   You should present in the safety report, clear links between the conclusions and:

(a)   the analysis of the risks, including the likelihoods of hazardous events and their consequences; and

(b)   the measures taken, technical or managerial, linked to ALARP, BATNEEC or inherent safety arguments.

112   Your arguments may be qualitative and focus on relevant good practice and sound engineering principles. They can also rely on generic arguments in preventing or limiting the consequences of a major accident based on a representative set of major accident scenarios. Several sources of good practice exist which are, in order of precedence:

(a)   prescriptive legislation;

(b)   regulatory guidance;

(c)   standards produced by standard-making organisations;

(d)   guidance agreed by an organisation representing a particular sector of industry; and

(e)   standard good practice adopted by a particular sector of industry.

113   If you use good practice as your sole justification of the chosen measures, then you should ensure that:

(a)   the practice is relevant to your situation;

(b)   any adopted standard is up to date and relevant; and

(c)   where a standard allows for more than one option for conformity, the chosen option makes the risks ALARP.

The issues that you have to consider, and some of the pitfalls, are discussed in more detail in paragraphs 44-63.

114   More complex situations may require the presentation of quantitative arguments coupled with cost benefit analysis in order to provide the justification that all measures necessary have been taken.

115   Quantitative risk assessment is also particularly valuable and appropriate when deciding the best option for a new facility. In such circumstances, it is not sufficient simply to assume that applying current good practice will ensure that the risks are ALARP. This is because with a new installation there are cost-effective opportunities to take account of technological advance, to seek inherently safer designs, and to take account of improvements in assessment methods and views on good practice.

116   Whatever additional measures are identified as being reasonably practicable, they should be implemented. The justification for rejecting possible risk-reduction measures needs to be well argued and supported with evidence.

117   The results of any risk assessment will be subject to uncertainty. Uncertainty in qualitative risk assessment arises from the validity of any assumptions made, the 'completeness' of the hazard identification, and views on the likelihoods of hazardous events and associated consequences.

118   Uncertainty in quantified risk analysis arises from assumptions, the extent that relevant data is complete and accurate, and how adequate and appropriate the models are. The greater the uncertainty, the greater the need for a conservative approach supported by strong qualitative arguments based on sound engineering judgement and relevant good practice.

119   In situations where good practice has yet to be established, collateral evidence from similar situations may be helpful. For example, if a novel design of a storage vessel is adopted, failure modes and likelihoods can be developed by taking account of what is known about these parameters for current designs.

120   The range of hazardous scenarios considered needs to be representative and suitable for emergency planning purposes. The consequences of catastrophic vessel failure and guillotine fracture of pipework should be considered, as well as more likely scenarios for loss of containment, such as flange failures or a release from a 50 mm aperture.

121   The worst case scenarios for people and the environment must be considered. The analysis of these should not be overly optimistic or pessimistic, as this could have resource implications for the emergency services. This means the consequence models and assumptions used need to be appropriate for the scale and nature of the hazards.

122   The levels of harm considered and the impact criteria/vulnerability models used must be suitable for predicting the extent of areas where people might be fatally or seriously injured, or require hospitalisation. For environmental impact assessment, corresponding levels of harm to the environment should be considered.

Writing the safety report

123   Remember that the COMAH Regulations require operators 'to take all measures necessary to prevent major accidents and limit their consequences'. When preparing the safety report, you should carefully examine the things that matter in your management of dangerous substances and major accident hazards on site. This means that, as you obtain information and analyse it, you should be looking for opportunities to make improvements in safety and to adopt them if you think they are necessary. You can report on your plans for these improvements in the safety report.

124   You should follow these steps when preparing your safety report:

(a)   gather information;

(b)   analyse the information to make the demonstrations;

(c)   act on the information if the analysis shows that improved safety measures are needed; and

(d)   present the information in a structured way to make the demonstrations very clear.

(a) Gathering information

125   There are four categories of information:

(a)   a description of the establishment, the dangerous substances on site and the nature of the surrounding environment;

(b)   information about the safety management systems;

(c)   information about the installations, particularly about major accident identification and the technical measures to ensure safety and protect the environment; and

(d)   information about the emergency response.

126   You need to gather the information from a number of sources. For example, you can find it among existing paperwork, such as standard operating procedures, plant and equipment records. Talking to managers, plant operators and employee representatives about what you need, and what they do, is very important.

127   You should be able to use a lot of the factual information from your CIMAH safety report, if you had one, although you should not simply submit it again under COMAH without reviewing it. This is because it is important that you are sure the information is sufficient for the demonstrations required, and that the arguments you use are presented in a clear and logical way in making those demonstrations. There may be legal licences that you have to prepare that can be used as a source of information, such as Integrated Pollution Control (IPC) authorisations.

(b) Analysing information to make the demonstrations

128   The section 'What does 'demonstration' mean?' (paragraphs 44-63) highlights what action has to be taken. Essentially, the demonstrations link information about:

(a)   'what can go wrong' to 'what measures the operator has taken to prevent it going wrong'; and

(b) 'whether those measures described are justified by showing a sufficiently systematic and rigorous process for making the decisions on whether the measures taken are all that are necessary.'

129 British and European standards, and HSE and the environment agencies' guidance are all benchmarks for good practice, ie what is appropriate. If the measures on site are not good enough, then action should be taken or planned to improve them. However, you are not expected to take retrospective action just because more modern plant would have different, perhaps better, controls. You should evaluate what you have, and decide if it is reasonably practicable (see Appendix 4 as to how this term is interpreted by the competent authority) to improve current systems.

130 If the site was subject to CIMAH, parts of the analysis may have already been done, so you need to demonstrate that you are continuing to do the right things to prevent major accidents. You need to ask: 'Why are we doing the things the way we are, and are these appropriate now and in the future for the major hazards identified?'

(c) Acting on information if the analysis shows that improved safety measures are needed

131 You need to act if, while gathering the information you need, you find that something is missing. For example, if your site does not have a major accident prevention policy (MAPP) in line with regulation 5 of COMAH, you need to prepare one for inclusion in the safety report. This is one of the ways that writing a safety report benefits an operator: things overlooked are discovered. Do not attempt to cover up or falsify your findings in order to pass the assessment by the competent authority. If you do, this will leave you open to prosecution.

(d) Presenting information in a structured way to make the demonstrations very clear

132 You need to provide information that is sufficient for the assessors to understand why you are doing things the way you are. You may refer to other documents if necessary. The competent authority may request more information during assessment, but don't be so brief that your arguments cannot be understood without intimate knowledge of the documents referenced.

133 It helps to be logical in your presentation. You should keep in mind that the competent authority is looking for certain demonstrations to be made, and for clear links to the COMAH requirements. In presenting the safety report, you should move from overview and progress to detail. You should describe things and then present the analysis and demonstration. The use of chapters, sections, numbering and appendices all help to make the text flow, and allow for cross-referencing.

134 You should use Schedule 4 Part 2 as the basis for deciding the minimum information necessary. This chapter describes how a safety report might be structured, and explains why this might be a useful structure. You are not required to lay your safety report out in the same order as the chapters in this book. However, if you do, it will make the assessors' job easier and quicker, and make discussions with you easier.

135 The assessors are technically competent, but may be unfamiliar with the site and some of its activities. You should use plain English and explanatory diagrams. Details should be included of any action that you intend to take as a result of writing the safety report. You should explain how such action will be included in existing safety, health and environmental improvement plans.

136 You should already know why you take your existing measures to prevent major accidents and limit their consequences. These reasons should be explained clearly and honestly as you make your demonstrations. If you have straightforward operations and have made decisions about the necessary measures, based on good industry practice, say so.

137 You should not over-complicate your safety report. However, the guidance in this book should help you to consider whether there are any gaps in your demonstration. For example,

there may be limits to the application of some of the standards you are relying on, which are different to the circumstances on your site.

138   Your safety report may be challenged by the competent authority during its assessment. Such challenges should ultimately result in a safer operation. There is no gain, however, in disguising poor practice with complex arguments.

139   You are not required to provide extensive detail when it is possible to reference other reports or studies you may have prepared. However, your safety report should present a sufficiently self-contained demonstration to enable an assessor to make professional judgements on your arguments. Remember, reference documents are a useful way of supporting your arguments but are not a substitute for the demonstrations required in the safety report.

140   Where you cross-refer to other documents for detail to support statements, you should include a summary of the contributions made by the referenced documents to your demonstration, and be prepared to provide copies on request.

141   Safety reports are open for public inspection. If the reference documents you use are proprietary documents and contain sensitive information, and if they form part of the safety report, then the arrangements for requesting confidentiality apply (see paragraph 77). If an assessor requests further information which includes proprietary documentation which is sensitive, then this information, even if it does not form part of the safety report, may still be open for members of the public to see. In this case, you may wish to have the material returned after the competent authority has finished with such documents.

Chapter 3

Descriptive information

Introduction

142   This chapter covers the type of general descriptive information that you need to include in the safety report about your establishment. This information ranges from details such as addresses and telephone numbers for setting up good communication channels with the competent authorities to information about the dangerous substances on site. You also need to include an overview of your establishment and details about the environment surrounding it.

Details to allow communication with the competent authority

143   Some basic facts are needed to help communication between you and the competent authority. This is not a requirement in COMAH, but is essential for the assessment process. You should include, as a minimum:

(a)   the name of the site operator;

(b)   if the operator is a company, the address of its registered office;

(c)   if the operator is a trading partnership, the names and addresses of all trading partners, together with the name and address under which the partnership operates;

(d)   the name and address of the establishment and, if necessary, the installation covered by the safety report; and

(e)   the name, address, telephone and fax number of a contact within the operator's organisation for communication about the safety report.

144   You could also usefully include in the safety report:

(a)   an e-mail address;

(b)   ordnance survey six-figure map references defining the location of the establishment; and

(c)   details of whether the operator is part of a larger group of companies.

Providing information about the dangerous substances in use

145   There are four types of detail in this section about the dangerous substances:

(a)   maximum quantities;

(b)   names;

(c)   physical and chemical behaviour; and

(d)   immediate and delayed harm to people and the environment.

The following paragraphs describe these in more detail.

(a) Maximum quantities

146   You should include in the safety report the maximum quantities of dangerous substances actually present, or likely to be present, on your site.

147   You should check whether you have any chemicals in the list of dangerous substances set out in COMAH. The quantities should be checked for each chemical you have which matches the list of named dangerous substances in Schedule 1 Part 2, or which meets the criteria as a dangerous substance, laid down in Schedule 1 Part 3 (see the guide to the Regulations[1]). When checking what chemicals you have on site, remember that they can be found as:

(a)   raw materials, intermediates, finished products, by-products, catalysts, fuel and wastes;

(b)   additives and individual constituents of preparations; and

(c)   substances produced during process excursions, or other unplanned but foreseeable events.

148 In your safety report, you should include an inventory of all dangerous substances at or above lower-tier and top-tier threshold quantities. Dangerous substances below these quantities should also be included, if they are capable, directly or indirectly, of being involved in a major accident. You should give a reason for omitting any other dangerous substances on your site from the report.

149 When calculating the maximum inventories, you should take into account fluctuations in business activity and any established quantity under the Planning (Hazardous Substances) Regulations 1992, as amended by the Planning (Control of Major-Accident Hazards) Regulations 1999 or the Town and Country Planning (Hazardous Substances) (Scotland) Regulations 1993 (which are being amended). If there are any other legal authorisations which refer to quantities, for example Integrated Pollution Prevention and Control Directive (IPPC) or Integrated Pollution Control (IPC), you need to take those into account too.

150 If your establishment has a large and variable number of different dangerous substances, such as in a warehouse, you can describe them by grouping them into representative categories, in line with Schedule 1 Part 3, when quantifying them. If you do this, explain and justify the basis for the groupings you have chosen.

151 Where a number of different dangerous substances are present at less than their qualifying quantity, you should show in your safety report how individual quantities have been aggregated together in accordance with the rules in the guide to the Regulations.[1]

152 Schedule 1 Part 1, paragraph 4 permits quantities of dangerous substances below 2% of their qualifying quantity to be ignored, for the purpose of calculating the total quantity, but only if you can demonstrate that they cannot be a source of a major accident elsewhere on site.

153 You must make that demonstration in your safety report if you want to use that part of the Regulations. So, if you state in your safety report that small quantities of dangerous substances have been ignored, you must go on to give a simple demonstration that they cannot be a source of a major accident on site.

154 In quoting quantities, it is best to use SI units of measurement, for example kgs and tonnes.

(b) Names

155 For each dangerous substance or class of dangerous substance you identify, including those present as impurities, additives or constituents of preparations, you should include in the safety report:

(a) its chemical name, for example propane or butane, and where appropriate, its common chemical name, for example LPG;

(b) identification of the substance, for example chlorine, or class of substances, for example poly chloro-di-benz dioxines, according to the IUPAC system of nomenclature;

(c) the CAS (see glossary) number for the substance or class of substances; and

(d) the concentration of any impurity or additive, and proportion of each constituent in a preparation.

156 You should also provide any additional useful information to help identify the dangerous substance.

157 For explosives, explosive articles or their process intermediates, you need to provide the following additional information:

(a) the name and description corresponding to the UN number assigned to the explosive under the Classification and Labelling of Explosives Regulations 1983, where applicable;

(b) which definition of an explosive in Part 3 of Schedule 1 to COMAH it falls within; and

(c) its behaviour on accidental initiation described in terms of hazard type as used in licences issued by HSE under the Explosives Act 1875.

(c) Physical and chemical behaviour

158 You should provide factual information concerning the physical and chemical behaviour of dangerous substances present on the establishment. Only detail those physical and chemical properties relevant to the various demonstrations you make later in the safety report.

159 Examples of the sort of information you could include are:

(a) flashpoint - by an identified method;

(b) ignition temperature;

(c) flammable limits;

(d) vapour pressure;

(e) density;

(f) boiling point;

(g) data on reactions;

(h) miscibility;

(i) partition coefficient;

(j) rates of decomposition; and

(k) data on sensitiveness of explosives.

160 You should present the properties in a clear and concise form using appropriate and consistent units of measurement, preferably following the SI system.

161 You need to consider and report on the behaviour of dangerous substances under all normal operating conditions, process upset conditions and foreseeable accident conditions. So you should report whether the chemical behaviour of the substance differs in a range of conditions which may include, for example:

(a) process operating pressures and temperatures during start-up, regeneration, normal process operation, turndown, or other designed mode;

(b) production of products, by-products, residues or intermediates as a result of normal operations or through foreseeable accidental conditions;

(c) behaviour of reactor fluids during and following a process upset;

(d) behaviour of stored materials under normal operation and following loss of utility, for example refrigerated storage and heated storage;

(e) contamination of products; and

(f) following loss of containment.

(d) Immediate and delayed harm to people and the environment

162 You should provide factual information concerning the known physical, chemical or toxicological characteristics of dangerous substances on the establishment, which may cause immediate or delayed harm to either people or to the environment. The information should include dangerous substances formed as a result of normal and abnormal conditions. You also need to give an indication of the hazards posed.

163 You should only present those characteristics relevant to the various demonstrations you make later in the safety report. The evidence presented should address both the short-term and long-term effects and may include, for example:

(a) health hazards such as irritation, asphyxiation, cancer or mutagenic damage;

(b) lethal concentrations;

(c) harm caused by fire or explosion; and

(d) effects on the environment, including building damage, the ecosystem and relevant sensitive species.

164 The information presented should consider the harmful effects on people and the environment, and also outline the routes to harm, for example via airborne discharge, seepage into groundwater, formation of an

explosive cloud, or accidental initiation of explosives giving rise to a fireball or blast. Characteristics such as bio-accumulation, persistence, dispersal mechanisms and known antagonistic or synergistic effects should also be considered.

165   You should present information concerning the acknowledged acceptable limits of exposure to the effects of the dangerous substances. Examples are control limits under the Control of Substances Hazardous to Health Regulations, LD50s and environmental quality standards (EQSs) (see glossary). The information presented should consider acceptable limits in terms of concentration, time of exposure, and any other relevant parameters.

166   You should provide appropriate references to scientific literature to justify the harmful effects, hazardous concentrations and acceptable limits you have presented. If there is little scientific knowledge of the effects, you should outline in the safety report your approach to evaluating the significance of that lack of knowledge and your policy for dealing with it.

> ### Providing information about the surrounding environment

167   You should provide factual information describing the environment surrounding the establishment. That includes the natural environment and the people in it, over, below and around the boundaries of the establishment. The extent of the area described should take account of hazard ranges of the worst case events you present later in the safety report.

168   It is best to include a map to a suitable scale, usually at least 1:10 000, showing the establishment and its surroundings. Separate maps may be required to identify the surrounding population and natural environment.

169   On the maps, it is important to indicate clearly:

(a)   the land use pattern, for example industry, agriculture, urban settlements and environmentally sensitive locations such as SSSIs, Ramsar sites;

(b)   the location of the most important buildings and infrastructures, for example hospitals, schools, other industrial sites, motorway and railway networks, stations and marshalling yards, airports and harbours; and

(c)   water extraction points as well as sewerage systems, since the latter can discharge pollutants many miles away from the site of the major accident.

170   Access routes to the establishment should be clearly indicated, as well as the escape routes from the establishment and other traffic routes significant for rescue and emergency operations. It may be necessary to have different scale maps if you are explaining long-distance effects from any major accidents.

171   There are five aspects of the surrounding environment which you need to consider:

(a)   people;

(b)   features contributing to a major accident;

(c)   the built environment;

(d)   the natural environment; and

(e)   external factors contributing to major accidents.

(a) People

172   There should be a description of the surrounding population. You could include, for example:

(a)   approximate numbers of residents;

(b)   estimated numbers of people who may use the area, for example those present at workplaces, present as tourists, or attending football matches or motorway services; and

(c)   groups of people who may be particularly vulnerable either on account of their sensitivity to the hazards in question, for example in schools and hospitals, or because of the population density.

173 You need to provide sufficient information to allow you and the competent authority to assess the indirect impact of a major accident on the public, for example as a result of the contamination of drinking water.

(b) Features contributing to a major accident

174 You need to think about and describe any features of the surrounding environment that may influence the impact of a major accident. Examples include:

(a) the topography, if it could have an effect on the dispersion of toxic or flammable gases or combustion products. This should include buildings, underground workings or other structures where appropriate, for example a pedestrian subway;

(b) historical local weather records, including wind speed, wind direction, atmospheric stability and rainfall, and the relevance of this information to the behaviour of releases of dangerous substances;

(c) the underlying and surrounding geology and hydrogeology, if it is appropriate to the consideration of a major accident;

(d) the surrounding water courses (under various flow conditions), underlying aquifers and any drinking water extraction points in relation to the dispersion of liquid contaminants or leachate from solids deposited on the surrounding land;

(e) surrounding water and land quality;

(f) sewage and rainwater systems, if they could be involved in the dispersal of liquid contaminants off site;

(g) tides and currents that might influence dispersion or accumulation, if marine or estuarine habitats are at risk; and

(h) features of the surroundings that may hinder emergency response or containment measures.

175 You should also consider consequential effects in which a dangerous substance causes the release of another substance which is polluting to the environment.

(c) The built environment

176 If the following structures may be vulnerable to the effects of a major accident, you should identify them:

(a) each listed building, major archaeological site and monument; and

(b) any sections of the infrastructure, including major transport routes or utilities, for example electricity, gas, telephone, water sewers and treatment plant.

177 The extent of the area described should take account of hazard ranges of the worst case events you present later in the safety report.

(d) The natural environment

178 You should describe the surrounding natural environment in enough detail to allow the significance of the impact of major accidents to be assessed by the competent authority. A detailed description of sensitive parts of the environment should be given. This should include:

(a) sites of special scientific interest (SSSI), whether they are special areas of conservation (SAC) or special protection areas (SPA), or Ramsar sites;

(b) marine nature reserves; and

(c) marine sensitive areas, under English Nature's or Scottish Natural Heritage's marine strategy.

179 The significance of these features in either a national or international context should be explained, for example plant life and animal life particularly at risk.

(e) External factors contributing to major accidents

180 You should provide sufficient factual information about the environment surrounding the establishment to allow the assessor to judge whether all external influences on major accidents have been included. The surrounding environment includes the natural environment over, below and around the boundaries of the establishment.

181 This information is required to allow the assessor to judge the adequacy of the description of possible major accident scenarios, and the events and conditions that might lead to them.

182 The physical environment surrounding the establishment may have an impact on events which cause possible major accidents. For example, when describing underlying geology, you should consider seismic events (earthquakes) and subsidence which might cause accidents.

183 The history of the land on which the establishment is located, together with its surroundings, may be significant when considering major accident causes. For example, the safety report should include information on the history of any mining or other mineral extraction activities, or any land reclamation in the area, which may lead to subsidence. You should also take into account previous land use which may be important in respect of contaminated land or water.

184 You should consider the historical evidence of other external events that might cause accidents, such as seismic events, flooding, and extreme weather conditions including temperature, rain, snow, wind, and lightning.

185 You need to take into account and describe any other activities in the area surrounding the establishment that might lead to, or exacerbate, a major accident. This information may include, for example:

(a) major hazard installations and pipelines in the area; *

(b) land use under the establishment, including current mining or mineral extraction activities;

(c) air traffic movements over and around the establishment, including civilian, military, fixed-wing aircraft and helicopters;

(d) transport activities that may have an impact, including shipping, major transport routes and dangerous substance movements;

(e) other human activities that might lead to major accidents, such as arson, vandalism, theft, and criminal damage;

(f) high-voltage overhead electric power distribution lines; and

(g) radio transmission masts in the area that produce fields which could interfere with safety control systems or communication systems, or initiate electro-explosive devices.

Providing an overview of the establishment, its activities and products

186 It is useful for the assessors if your safety report gives an overview of the establishment, its activities and products. An overview is a general outline, without extensive detail, to set the context for the reader. The overview could include:

(a) the installations;

(b) the major accident scenarios;

(c) the measures for protection and intervention;

(d) the interrelationship between different installations; and

* In so far as is obvious to you. The competent authority will inform you if there are any establishments adjacent to yours which increase the likelihood or consequences of a major accident. Once this is done, you have a duty under COMAH to exchange information about major accident hazards.

(e) the historical development of activities and production.

187 You are not specifically required by COMAH to give an overview, but it would be helpful to inspectors assessing your report.

188 However, you should include scaled plans or maps, plus descriptions, which clearly set out the internal geography of the establishment as a whole. The information should include, for example:

(a) location of installations with major hazard potential. If you are doing an overview first, it is not necessary to describe the features of those installations in any depth, for example plant, pipework, control rooms and explosive process areas. That can be done later;

(b) location of all other installations, including those that do not contain a dangerous substance, with an outline in general terms of what activity occurs there, or what substance(s) is present there;

(c) numbers and locations of people, for example in control rooms, office blocks, canteens and security huts. This needs to take into account foreseeable fluctuations which could be due to shift working, maintenance activities, contractors or visitors;

(d) location of any activities which relate to the major accident scenarios given in the safety report (the activities themselves can be described in more detail after the overview), for example chlorine tanker filling points and forward emergency control sites;

(e) location of any key abatement systems preventing or containing major accidents, such as drainage and firewater retention, gas cleaning or liquid treatment works, explosive buildings traverses or mounds important for the protection of people and the environment;

(f) location of any key control systems, such as computer control systems or isolation systems;

(g) location of roads, railways or docks, entrances to the establishment (including those for emergency vehicles only) or any other features relevant to the major accident scenarios in the safety report, such as flares or other open sources of ignition;

(h) sources of, and key features in, essential utilities which may be relevant to the prevention or containment of a major accident, and details of any redundancy, diversity and segregation, for example instrument air, steam or electrical networks;

(i) matters relevant to emergency response, such as firewater supply, escape routes and communication systems;

(j) systems for monitoring and detecting toxic products in air, water or sewers;

(k) systems for fire detection and monitoring potentially explosive atmospheres; and

(l) systems for monitoring access and for detecting intruders.

Information about the management measures to prevent major accidents

189   This chapter gives guidance about how to present your major accident prevention policy (MAPP) and information about the safety management systems (SMS) for implementing it.

190   The chapter will help you understand:

(a)   what should be in a MAPP; and

(b)   the required elements of an SMS for implementing the MAPP.

191   Some of the information here may not be relevant to your own establishment. However, your safety report should demonstrate that your MAPP and your SMS are adequate in the context of the major accident hazards at your site. The measures that you describe for preventing and limiting major accidents (discussed in more detail in Chapters 6 and 7) will show how well the MAPP and SMS have been put into effect.

192   The chapter also briefly deals with the management organisation for alert and intervention, however this is dealt with more fully in Chapter 7 which is concerned with emergency response.

> *Describing the aims of your safety management system (SMS), and how it takes account of all the processes mentioned in your safety report*

Setting the scene - elements of the safety management system

193   Your SMS is just one part of your overall management system, which may in turn be part of a management system for a larger company or group of companies. Your SMS may also be integrated within other management systems on site, such as the quality management system. For the safety report, you need to narrow this down to the information that is relevant.

194   The SMS described in your safety report should cover those parts of your general management arrangements which relate to the purpose and implementation of the MAPP. It should also describe those risk management control systems which are important to the control of major hazards.

195   This means that you do not need to describe your entire SMS, because it extends to matters beyond major accident prevention, for example occupational health and manual handling. Your safety report needs to only provide an account of your general management arrangements for determining and implementing the MAPP, and descriptions of those management risk control systems which are important for preventing major accidents and limiting the consequences for people and the environment.

196   Effective management involves agreeing objectives, defining a plan to achieve those objectives, formulating detailed work to implement the plan, checking the outcomes against the plan, and then planning and taking appropriate corrective action. The management of major accident hazards is no exception to these general rules.

197   The HSE publication HSG65 *Successful health and safety management*[8] describes the essential elements for effective management of health and safety based on an analysis of companies which succeed in achieving high standards. The model describing the interrelationship between these elements is reproduced in Figure 1.

Figure 1 Management arrangements for successful health and safety management

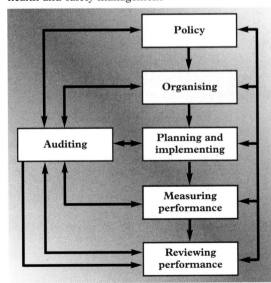

Figure 2 Three-component management model adapted to the management of major hazards

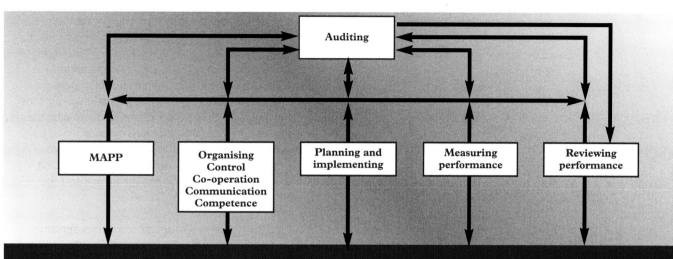

KEY RISK CONTROL SYSTEMS

OPERATIONAL CONTROL	MANAGEMENT OF CHANGE	PLANNING FOR EMERGENCIES
Construction and commissioning	People	Internal emergency plans
Operation	Plant	Mitigatory measures
Safety during maintenance (inc permits to work)	Design	Inspection, test and maintenance of mitigatory measures
Selection/management of contractors	Processes	Emergency response training
Inspection, test and maintenance	Process variables	Testing of emergency plans
Decommissioning	Materials	
	Equipment	
	Procedures	
	Software	
	Design changes	
	External circumstances	

PREVENTION AND MITIGATION MEASURES

Design of plant and controls	Maintenance
Alarms and emergency systems	Plant inspection
Control of contractors	Emergency plan
Permit to work	Site emergency facilities
Safe operating procedures	Information to CEPO
	Information to the public

198 The elements are a mixture of management arrangements, systems which determine how particular risks are to be controlled (risk control systems) and workplace precautions. This three-component model is described in Chapter 4 of *Successful health and safety management.*[8]

199 The elements of an SMS for implementing the MAPP are listed at Schedule 2 of the COMAH Regulations. They are consistent with the *Successful health and safety management*[8] model, and can also be viewed in terms of the management arrangements and key risk control systems illustrated in Figure 2. The guidance which follows is set out in a way which makes it clear where the elements of the SMS fit within the model, and the framework illustrated at Figure 2.

200 By way of example, Figure 3 illustrates the model, and framework described in Figure 2, as applied to the key risk control system for permits to work. It can be applied equally to other risk control systems, and it may help to have this framework in mind when you describe the key risk control systems in your safety report.

201 There are alternative models describing the interrelationship between the key elements of a successful SMS. You are free to choose these alternatives when describing your SMS in company documents. You are not legally obliged to present information about your MAPP and SMS using the *Successful health and safety management*[8] format as set out in this chapter. However, if you do, the assessment of your safety report by the competent authority will be easier.

Figure 3 Example of headings and content for describing a risk control system in a safety report

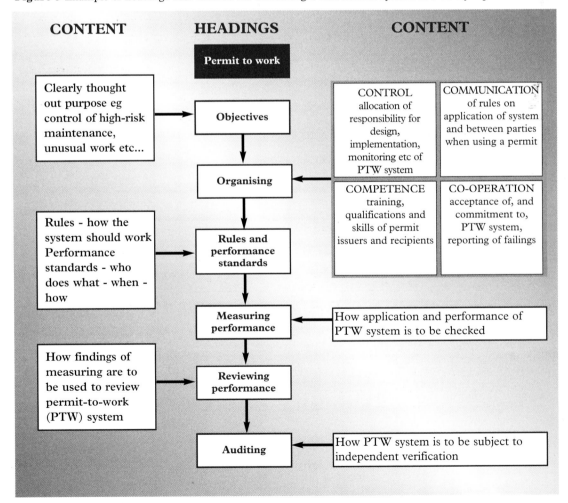

202   Your general management arrangements may include independent third party certification such as BS EN ISO 9001[9] for quality management and/or ISO 14001 for environmental management, and you should mention these in your safety report.

203   Adoption of these, or similar standards, does not automatically lead to appropriate attention to health and safety in the workplace. However, continued certification indicates that certain management procedures, directly related to managing health and safety matters relevant to major accidents, are in place, for example training, preparation, issue and control of instructions, and management of records. It also indicates that certain management procedures have been found to be operating satisfactorily over a period of time.

204   Management will also have shown commitment by providing resources to a business function with many aspects similar to those required for the effective management of health and safety. Although BS 8800 is not required to follow a third party certification system, it is consistent with the guidance in the publication HSG65. Again, reference to following this standard is a good indication that certain management systems are in place, but a demonstration is still required in the safety report of how these prevent or limit major accidents.

Overall aim

205   Concerning the management arrangements, your aim should be to ensure that your safety report:

(a)   contains a MAPP;

(b)   demonstrates that there is an SMS for implementing the MAPP;

(c)   demonstrates that the MAPP and the rest of the SMS have been put into effect, taking into account all that you have said in the rest of the safety report; and

(d)   demonstrates that all the measures necessary have been taken to prevent major accidents and to limit their consequences for people and the environment.

206   Your safety report will also include descriptions of a series of outcomes which are themselves determined or influenced by your SMS, such as the technical precautions and predictive elements. This information helps to demonstrate that the MAPP and SMS have been put into effect.

207   You should aim to show in your safety report that you have a system for delivering the desired outcomes. For example, one important outcome under the heading 'Competence' would be that people with key roles in the control of major accident hazards are competent in relation to their duties.

208   You shouldn't just mention people's relevant qualifications here. Rather, you should show that you have a system in place for providing and maintaining appropriate levels of management and employee competence. This is important. You need to show that you have a systematic approach for achieving important outcomes, and that the outcomes have not come about by chance or in an ad hoc way.

The major accident prevention policy (MAPP)

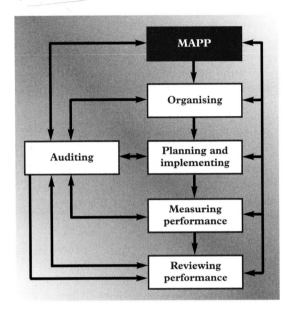

209 Your MAPP in the safety report should include:

(a) a statement showing your company's commitment to achieving high standards of safety and environmental performance as well as an indication that the necessary resources will be made available;

(b) a recognition that the nature of your company's activities gives rise to major accident hazards for employees, contractors, visitors, members of the public, and the natural and built environment as appropriate, and therefore that your company has obligations to employees, neighbours and the environment;

(c) statements explaining your company's overall aims and principles of action in relation to the control of major accidents. Without a clear policy setting out what you aim to achieve, delivering the necessary control is likely to be ad hoc; and

(d) a commitment to provide and maintain a management system which addresses the following issues in the context of your site:

(i) the roles and responsibilities of those involved in the management of major hazards at all levels in the organisation, including contractors where appropriate, and the provision of training to meet identified training needs;

(ii) the arrangements for systematically identifying major hazards arising from normal and abnormal operation, and the assessment of their likelihood and severity;

(iii) the arrangements and procedures for safe operation, including maintenance of plant, processes, equipment and temporary stoppages;

(iv) the arrangements for planning modifications to, or the design of, new installations, processes and storage facilities;

(v) the arrangements for identifying foreseeable emergencies by systematic analysis, and for preparing, testing and reviewing emergency plans in response to such emergencies;

(vi) the arrangements for the ongoing assessment of compliance with the objectives set out in the MAPP and SMS, and the mechanisms for investigation and corrective action in the event of failing to achieve the stated objectives. These should include your system for reporting major accidents and near misses, particularly those involving failure of protective measures, and their investigation and follow-up on the basis of lessons learnt; and

(vii) the arrangements for periodic systematic assessment of the MAPP and the effectiveness and suitability of the SMS, the documented review of performance of the MAPP and SMS, and their updating by senior management.

210   The MAPP should be signed and dated by an appropriate director or senior executive to signify that it is truly the policy of the 'controlling minds' of the organisation.

211   By including it as part of the safety report, the report shows that the MAPP has been established in writing.

212   Corporate health and safety policies under the Health and Safety at Work etc Act 1974 can not be used as MAPPs unless they include your aims and principles of action for the prevention of major accidents both to people and the environment.

Organising

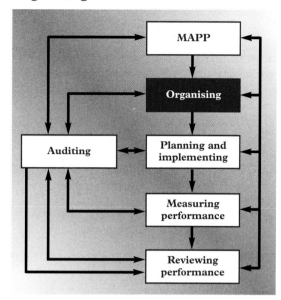

213   The SMS, as described in your safety report, should reflect the top-down commitment, environmental awareness and safety culture of your organisation. It should then describe how this is translated into the direct responsibilities of people involved in the management of major hazards at all levels within your organisation.

214   *Successful health and safety management*[8] categorises the activities necessary for successfully organising health and safety into four elements (the 4Cs):

(a)   control;

(b)   competence;

(c)   co-operation; and

(d)   communication.

Details on what information should be included in your safety report are given in the following paragraphs.

(a) Control

215   To demonstrate that your SMS fits in with your overall management system, your safety report should include suitable summaries outlining the allocation of roles and responsibilities for all aspects of the management of major hazards. These should be illustrated, where appropriate, with organisational charts.

Allocation of roles and responsibilities

216   You should include descriptions in the safety report to show that roles and responsibilities for the management of major accident hazards have been properly allocated at the right levels within the organisation, to ensure top-down commitment and a positive safety and environment culture.

217   Responsibilities for developing the MAPP and providing the resources, for example, should be allocated at senior management level. Responsibilities for implementing and maintaining particular control measures might rest at lower levels of management.

218   Your safety report should confirm that the control of major accident hazards is a management function, and that any safety and environmental professionals act in support of line management.

Clear definition of all responsibilities

219   Your safety report should show that the responsibilities of everyone involved in the management of major hazards have been clearly defined, so that employees and other people involved know who is responsible for each relevant aspect. For example, you may refer to other documents, such as performance standards which set out rules for who does what, how, when and with what expected result. It is not necessary, however, to include copies of job descriptions.

220   You should describe the responsibilities allocated to key managers and post holders at all levels. Depending on your company's management structure, you need to identify the key managers and post holders for each of the following responsibilities:

(a)   providing resources, including human resources, for developing, implementing and maintaining the SMS;

(b)   identifying major hazards and assessing associated risks during the life cycle of the installation;

(c)   ensuring that employees, contractors and others are aware of the major accident hazards, and are competent in the safety systems;

(d)   designing new installations and planning modifications;

(e)   identifying, recording and following up corrective and improvement actions;

(f)   controlling abnormal situations and emergencies;

(g)   identifying relevant training needs, providing training and evaluating its effectiveness;

(h)   implementing the key risk control systems necessary for the control of major hazards;

(i)   co-ordinating the implementation of the SMS and reporting to senior management; and

(j)   monitoring performance and carrying out audits and reviews.

Allocation of sufficient resources

221   Your safety report should show how your company has allocated sufficient resources to implement the MAPP. For example, you could include brief explanations of how resources, including human and financial resources, are determined and allocated for the overall management of major accident hazards.

222   Explanations should be provided of how key risk control systems are resourced, and of the arrangements for filling key posts.

223   Your systems for identifying absences of key personnel, and for arranging competent cover, should be explained. You should also indicate how your company ensures that levels of supervision are appropriate to the tasks being undertaken, the degree of instruction provided and the proficiency of the people undertaking the work.

Appraisal and accountability of personnel

224　Your safety report should show that appraisals are carried out on the performance of people having a role to play in the management of major accident hazards, and that they are held accountable for their performance. To do this, your safety report could, for example:

(a)　explain how the responsibilities for management of major accident hazards are made clear to job holders, for example in job descriptions or other documents;

(b)　refer to any system you have for formal personal performance review and appraisal, which sets objectives relevant to the control of major accident hazards and measures the extent to which objectives are achieved;

(c)　give information about procedures for identifying and taking action on failures to achieve satisfactory performance;

(d)　refer to any disciplinary procedures and incentive or reward schemes;

(e)　summarise the arrangements for setting performance standards and targets for line managers.

(b) Competence

225　Your safety report should show that your company has a system in place for providing and maintaining appropriate levels of management and employee competence.

226　Managers and employees need to have the necessary knowledge, skills and experience to be able to meet their responsibilities for the control of major accident hazards. Your safety report should show that people having key roles in the control of major accident hazards are competent in relation to their responsibilities.

227　Your safety report could, for example:

(a)　outline the arrangements for the selection, recruitment, training and placement of employees and managers at all levels including, where relevant, contractors;

(b)　describe the arrangements you have for determining the relevant qualifications, skills and experience required for post holders, teams or groups having a significant role to play in the management of major hazards. The descriptions would cover relevant posts at all levels and in all relevant functions, for example senior executives, key line managers, specialists, plant operators and maintenance staff and, where appropriate, managers, supervisors and employees of contractors and sub-contractors;

(c)　refer to the arrangements for identifying the training needs of all those having a role to play in the control of major accident hazards, including their deputies, from directors or senior executives, down to operators and including contractors and their employees. These arrangements might cover the identification of training needs arising from recruitment, staff changes (including changes to staff employed by contractors), changes to plant, processes or working practices, or from the need to maintain and enhance competence;

(d)　explain the arrangements for communication, including providing relevant information, instruction and training. These would include arrangements for induction training, professional training, job specific training, and refresher training;

(e)　outline the relevant profession, discipline, trade and training for each individual who has an important role in your company's systems for preventing and containing major accidents;

(f)　indicate what arrangements you have for the validation and evaluation of training; and

(g)　refer to your arrangements for providing specialist and expert advice, whether from in-house professionals or from external sources.

(c) Co-operation

228 Your safety report should show that your company has systems for involving employees in the control of major accident hazards.

229 Senior managers cannot manage major accident hazards on their own. The commitment, co-operation and active participation of employees at all levels are essential for success. There is also a need to tap the knowledge and experience of employees at all levels, including those of local safety and environment professionals, because they can identify problems and help to provide solutions.

230 Formal systems are needed to secure the continued participation, commitment and involvement of employees in the safety and environment effort in general, and in the management of major accident hazards in particular. Involvement of employees will not happen unless your company adopts a structured approach to securing their participation.

231 If a person working under your control and direction is treated as self-employed for tax and national insurance purposes, they may nevertheless be treated as your employee for health and safety purposes. You may need therefore to take appropriate action to protect them. If you do not wish to employ workers on this basis, you should seek legal advice. Ultimately each case can only be decided on its own merits by a court of law.

232 As appropriate, your safety report should, for example:

(a) summarise how your company has set about developing a culture which encourages the active participation of the workforce, including contractors and their employees, in the health, safety and environment effort;

(b) explain how the workforce is involved in consultative bodies, health, safety and environment committees, safety circles and safety teams;

(c) describe how your company encourages and supports employee or safety representatives;

(d) outline the arrangements for upward reporting of information relevant to the control of major hazards; and

(e) refer to the mechanisms which your company has in place for securing the participation of employees in key activities such as:

   (i) setting standards relevant to the control of major accident hazards;

   (ii) the design and procurement of new equipment including the human machine interface to ensure human factors and usability are taken into account;

   (iii) devising, reviewing and revising operating procedures and emergency systems, and the relevant instructions, for the control of major accident hazards;

   (iv) hazard studies, for example HAZOP, and risk assessments;

   (v) performance-measuring activities including accident, incident and near-miss investigations; and

   (vi) audit and review.

233 Your safety report should show that your company has arrangements in place for co-operating with, and securing the co-operation of, other organisations with key roles to play in the prevention and limitation of major accidents. Co-operating with them and securing their co-operation is essential because not everything is within your control.

234 You could, for example, outline your arrangements for co-operating with:

(a) operators of other establishments which might be affected by the major accident hazards;

(b) contractors and their employees;

(c) the emergency services;

(d) county and other authorities responsible for the preparation and maintenance of external emergency plans;

(e) local authorities;

(f) enforcing authorities;

(g) employers' associations; and

(h) any other relevant bodies.

(d) Communication

235 Your safety report should show that your company has arrangements for gathering information needed for the control of major accident hazards from external sources. Unless your company is able to obtain important information about these issues from external sources, it cannot manage major accident hazards properly, or achieve compliance with the relevant legal requirements.

236 This means your safety report should describe how you ensure that important safety information is obtained, such as changes in legislation, developments in technical standards and management practices, information about incidents with major accident potential occurring elsewhere in the world. Sources might include:

(a) enforcing authorities;

(b) professional bodies;

(c) industry associations;

(d) emergency services;

(e) other companies; and

(f) local authorities.

237 Your report should also explain your arrangements for internally communicating information important for the control of major accident hazards. Effective communication from the top down, bottom up and horizontally within an organisation, including any corporate functions, is essential for the successful management of major accident hazards.

238 This means your safety report should include, for example:

(a) an outline of how you communicate to employees, contractors and others: the MAPP; the values and beliefs underlying it; and the procedures and risk control systems important for the management of major hazards;

(b) a description of the arrangements by which relevant plans, standards, procedures and risk control systems important for the management of major accident hazards are communicated within your organisation;

(c) explanations of how information from relevant performance monitoring and auditing activities is gathered and communicated;

(d) descriptions of how comments, suggestions and ideas for improvement from individuals and teams are collected, dealt with and acted upon;

(e) explanations of how senior and line managers show their commitment to the MAPP through their visible behaviour, for example by participating in appropriate active monitoring activities, taking part in accident and incident investigations, participating in and, where appropriate, chairing the meetings of safety committees;

(f) reference to the arrangements for written communications important for the management of major accident hazards, for example systems for:

(i) recording and communicating the written MAPP statement;

(ii) documenting the roles and responsibilities for implementing the MAPP;

(iii) documenting and publishing relevant plans and objectives within the organisation;

(iv) documenting key risk control systems and associated procedures, rules and instructions, for example in safety manuals;

(v) recording and publishing progress towards achievement of relevant plans and objectives;

(vi) recording and publishing information on safety and environmental performance;

(vii) revising, updating, distributing and controlling relevant documents; and

(viii) co-ordinating the transfer of guidance and information relevant to safety and environmental issues;

(g) an outline of how formal and informal face-to-face discussions on issues relating to the control of major accident hazards take place:

(i) routine management meetings at all levels, including board level, at which important safety and environment-related issues form an agenda item;

(ii) team briefings at which important safety and environment-related information is cascaded, and at which feedback from employees is obtained;

(iii) meetings of safety committees;

(iv) wash-up meetings following rehearsals of emergency plans;

(v) planning and liaison meetings with contractors; and

(vi) toolbox talks.

239 Your safety report should say what arrangements you have for communicating information related to the control of major accident hazards to external organisations.

240 The report should also outline, for example, your arrangements for communicating with:

(a) other establishments in the vicinity, including exchanging information about major accident hazards and emergency plans;

(b) the emergency services and local authorities in relation to emergency plans;

(c) county and other authorities responsible for the preparation and maintenance of external emergency plans;

(d) people off site who are liable to be affected by a major accident, by supplying them with the information required under regulation 14 of COMAH, and making it available to the public; and

(e) relevant enforcing authorities including HSE and the environment agencies.

Organisation of the alert and intervention for emergencies

241 Your safety report should describe the organisation of the alert and intervention in the event of a major accident. The principles of the organisation of a risk control system which have been described in paragraphs 213-240, apply equally to the organisation of the alert and intervention for emergencies. The details of what should be included under this specific heading, and what should be achieved, are described in Chapter 7.

Planning and implementing

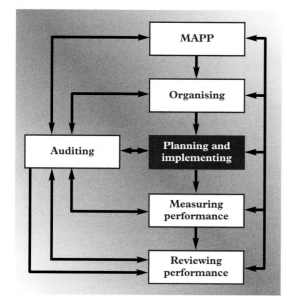

242 Arrangements are needed to establish and implement a MAPP. This means a systematic approach to planning, in order to decide where you are now in relation to the control of major hazards, where you want to be and how you are going to get there.

243 You should describe your arrangements for identifying major accident hazards, assessing risks and determining the measures needed to control the risks.

244 You should describe your procedures for identifying gaps and weaknesses in your management arrangements, key risk control systems, and those physical controls and workplace precautions which are important for the control of major hazards.

245 There should be systems in place to:

(a) identify hazards and assess risks;

(b) identify areas for improvement; and

(c) select priorities and schedule improvements.

246 These are discussed in the following paragraphs.

Hazard identification and risk assessment

247 Management of major accident hazards needs to be an active and continuing process. Arrangements for systematic identification of major hazards, risk assessment and choice of necessary control measures are therefore vital. In your safety report you should, for example:

(a) refer to procedures for identifying and evaluating the major accident hazards arising from the operator's activities, and from the substances and materials purchased, stored, processed or produced;

(b) outline your arrangements for deciding on the skills and knowledge required and, where appropriate, the team approach needed to provide the necessary range of theoretical and practical knowledge to implement appropriate hazard identification and risk assessment procedures;

(c) explain the formal hazard identification and risk assessment techniques (see paragraph 293 and following) actually used at each stage of the process plant or storage facility's life cycle. A well-structured safety report would include discussion of:

(i) selection of the site, and the siting of buildings within the establishment;

(ii) plant and process design and modification, including what methods of hazard identification and risk assessment were used at the time the plant and processes were designed; it is important that you check that your HAZOP assessment covers the environmental effects as well as the health and safety of people;

(iii) construction, installation and commissioning;

(iv) start-up, steady-state running and shutdown under normal and abnormal conditions;

(v)   routine and non-routine maintenance;

(vi)   incidents and possible emergencies, including those arising from component or materials failure, external events, human factors and failures of the SMS itself; and

(vii)   decommissioning, abandonment and disposal;

(d)   refer to the techniques used to identify the hazards and assess the risks arising from external factors, such as:

(i)   intrinsic location hazards, for example contaminated land, mine workings;

(ii)   abnormal temperatures, fire, lightning strike, seismic activity, wind, subsidence and landslip, flood, snow loading, and aircraft and missile impact;

(iii)   transport, civil engineering and lifting activities;

(iv)   neighbouring activities; and

(v)   malevolent or unauthorised action including trespass;

(e)   describe how your arrangements for risk assessment take account of human factors, including human behaviour and reliability, and the potential for human error in relation to safety critical activities;

(f)   describe how the outcomes of hazard identification and risk assessment are used to determine the physical control measures and the risk control systems needed for the prevention and limitation of major accidents. In particular, you should describe any criteria used to judge the significance of the residual risks when control measures are implemented and to show that these risks are 'as low as reasonably practicable' (ALARP).* These are fundamental to your justification that all measures necessary are being taken, which are discussed in detail in Chapter 6. This justification should include your consideration of ways of eliminating hazards, reducing their scale, and other means for reducing the associated risks, in other words, avoiding or reducing the likelihood of an event occurring and limiting the consequences. Your approach should embrace current thinking on inherently safer design options, on relevant good practice, and on engineering and procedural standards;

(g)   describe how you target any risk assessment so that it is both suitable and sufficient (see Chapter 5); and

(h)   describe your approach to eliminating possible hazardous events from your risk analysis.

Identifying areas for improvement

248   Your safety report should show that these systems are in place and how improvements are planned. It could include, for example:

(a)   how areas for improvement, in relation to the control of major accidents, are identified; and

(b)   references to your current improvement plans to show that they are relevant to the control of major hazards.

Selecting priorities and scheduling improvements

249   Your safety report should show that your company has systems both for setting priorities to achieve the objectives of the MAPP, and for scheduling necessary improvement work in relation to the control of major accident hazards. It could include, for example:

(a)   indications of how priorities are decided, and how they are based on considerations of hazard or risk;

(b)   reference to current improvement plans with a suitable explanation of the basis on which priorities have been decided;

* Appendix 4 gives the competent authority's view on ensuring risks are ALARP.

(c) explanations of how improvement work relevant to the control of major accident hazards is scheduled, how the work is resourced, co-ordinated and allocated to individuals or teams to carry out, and how timescales for completion are set;

(d) reference to the operator's current improvement plans, to illustrate how work has been scheduled; and

(e) reference to any current backlogs of improvement work, including overdue maintenance schedules indicating how these are being tackled.

Key risk control systems

250 HSE's book *Successful health and safety management*[8] explains what risk control systems are. These are aimed at the control of particular categories of risk, and the concept is illustrated in Figure 2.

251 The COMAH Regulations specifically require your SMS to address three important sets of risk control systems (the key risk control systems) namely:

(a) operational control;

(b) management of change; and

(c) planning for emergencies.

252 Operational control, management of change and emergency planning each cover a wide range of risks. The following guidance may not be relevant to all establishments, so use it selectively to demonstrate that the necessary measures which have been taken are adequate in relation to the major accident hazards at your own site.

253 In outlining these key risk control systems in your safety report, you should say how each system works and not just give their outcomes. You should try and describe each system in terms of its purpose, organisation, standards, performance measurement, audit and review. In doing this, you will reflect the structure in Figure 3.

(a) Operational control

254 You should include descriptions of the risk control systems relevant to each stage of the life cycle of the plant, processes or storage facilities in question. These include systems for each of the following stages, as appropriate:

(a) construction and commissioning of plant, processes, equipment and facilities;

(b) operation of plant and processes, including as appropriate:

(i) start-up;

(ii) steady-state running;

(iii) normal shutdown; and

(iv) detection of departures from normal operating conditions and responses to them, including emergency shutdown, and temporary and special operations;

(c) safe operation under maintenance conditions, including:

(i) carrying out risk assessment for decontamination and maintenance work; and

(ii) generating safe methods of working for maintenance and using permit-to-work systems to control it;

(d) selection and management of contractors;

(e) inspection, test and maintenance of plant, equipment and facilities; and

(f) decommissioning of plant, processes, equipment and facilities.

(b) Management of change

255 Absences of, and failings in, systems for change management have been significant

contributory causes to major accidents. It is essential that your company has in place an effective and reliable system for managing change.

256 Your safety report should show that you have adopted and implemented procedures for planning modifications to, or the design of, new installations, processes or storage facilities. It should include descriptions of:

(a) your system for planning and controlling all changes in:

    (i) staffing levels;

    (ii) people;

    (iii) plant;

    (iv) processes and process variables;

    (v) materials;

    (vi) equipment;

    (vii) procedures;

    (viii) software;

    (ix) design; and

    (x) external circumstances which are capable of affecting the control of major accident hazards, where appropriate;

(b) the concepts used for the design of new plant or processes explaining how:

    (i) responsibilities for authorising and initiating design of new plant are being allocated;

    (ii) proposed designs for new plant are identified and documented;

    (iii) safety and environmental implications of proposed new plant are identified, assessed, and prioritised, including how inherent safety and ergonomics issues are considered in the early stages of design;

    (iv) safety and environmental control measures seen as necessary as a result of new plant, including the provision of information and training and amendment of procedures, are defined, documented and implemented; and

    (v) post-implementation checks and reviews are carried out and corrective action taken;

(c) how your management of change system covers permanent, temporary and urgent changes;

(d) the management of change system explaining, as appropriate, how:

    (i) decisions about what constitutes a significant change, within the meaning of regulation 8(4), are made;

    (ii) change has been defined;

    (iii) responsibilities for authorising and initiating change have been allocated;

    (iv) proposed changes are identified and documented;

    (v) safety and environmental implications of proposed changes are identified, assessed and prioritised;

    (vi) safety and environmental control measures seen as necessary as a result of change, including the provision of information and training and amendment of procedures, are defined, documented and implemented;

    (vii) post-change checks and reviews are carried out and corrective action implemented; and

    (viii) the involvement of third parties, such as contractors, is managed.

(c) Planning for emergencies

257 The matters described in this section are also relevant to Chapter 7, and you may choose to include them in that part of your safety report which specifically deals with the demonstration relating to providing an on-site emergency plan.

258 Your safety report should show that your company has arrangements in place to identify foreseeable emergencies by means of systematic analysis, and that you prepare, test and review emergency plans.

259 In your safety report you should describe your procedures for:

(a) systematically identifying the consequences of any major accidents that could occur;

(b) preparing, reviewing, testing and updating emergency plans, at suitable intervals of no longer than three years. The procedures should take account of the need to review the emergency plans in the light of:

(i) the lessons learned from emergency exercises, including how humans respond and behave in such situations;

(ii) changes at your establishment; and

(iii) new technical knowledge, and information concerning the response to major accidents;

(c) taking account of likely human behaviour and response under emergency conditions, when developing emergency plans.

Measuring performance

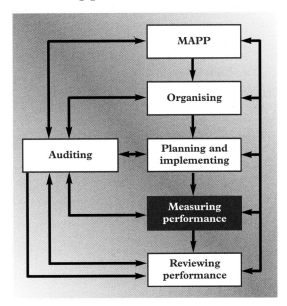

260 Your company should devise, implement and maintain procedures to ensure that safety and environmental performance is monitored and compared with the objectives set by your MAPP and any other standards which you have set for yourselves. This should include procedures for:

(a) active monitoring - determining whether plans and objectives are being achieved, and whether the arrangements for controlling risks are being implemented before an incident or accident occurs; and

(b) reactive monitoring - reporting and investigating failures which have led to incidents and near misses.

Active monitoring

261 A low accident or incident rate over a period of years is no guarantee that risks are being effectively controlled. This is particularly so in organisations involved in major hazard activities, where the probability of an accident may be low but where the consequences could be extremely serious.

262 In this type of organisation, the historical incidence of reported accidents alone can be an unreliable indicator of safety or environmental performance, and can lead to

complacency. Effective arrangements for active monitoring are essential for operators of major hazard establishments.

263 Your safety report should show that your company has adopted and implemented procedures for the ongoing assessment of compliance with the objectives set by the MAPP and SMS. It could include, for example:

(a) outlines of your active monitoring arrangements, important for the prevention and limitation of major accidents, for example:

   (i) identification, inspection and test of critical plant, equipment, controls and instrumentation;

   (ii) assessment of compliance with training, instructions, safe operating procedures and working practices;

   (iii) monitoring progress in achieving specific objectives deriving from the MAPP and allocated to individuals or teams under the operator's safety improvement plans;

   (iv) periodic examination of documents to check that standards aimed at maintaining and developing the SMS are complied with; and

   (v) arrangements under which managers at the appropriate level carry out checks on the quality of the monitoring activities performed by their staff;

(b) description of any behavioural or staff attitude surveys you use as part of a systematic examination of the safety culture within your organisation; and

(c) explanations of how you ensure that the active monitoring effort is proportional to the risk, for example that decisions about which items of plant, equipment and instrumentation, and which procedures and activities should be monitored, at what frequency and in what depth, are based on considerations of the risk.

Reactive monitoring

264 Reactive monitoring provides the opportunity to learn and to improve. Your safety report should show that your company has adopted and implemented a system for reporting major accidents and near misses, particularly those involving failure of the protective measures for the control of major accident hazards.

265 Your safety report should include descriptions of the arrangements which your company has in place for ensuring that the following incidents are recognised and reported to management:

(a) major accidents as defined in COMAH;

(b) other relevant injuries and cases of ill health;

(c) other significant events leading to loss or environmental harm;

(d) incidents, including individual behaviour, with the potential for harm, loss or environmental damage, particularly those with the potential for major accidents;

(e) hazardous conditions; and

(f) weaknesses or omissions in those risk control systems which are important for the prevention and limitation of major accidents.

Investigation and response

266 To learn from the results of active and reactive monitoring, you need systems for investigation. These are to determine the immediate and underlying causes of failure. This information should then be used to determine the necessary corrective action.

267 Your safety report should show that your company has adopted and implemented mechanisms for investigation and taking corrective action:

(a)   in cases of non-compliance with the objectives set by the MAPP; and

(b)   in relation to major accidents and near misses.

268   You might support this with, for example, descriptions of the arrangements for:

(a)   early evaluation to identify immediate risks;

(b)   taking prompt action on immediate risks;

(c)   deciding the level and nature of investigation, for example based on considerations of potential rather than actual outcome;

(d)   determining the immediate causes; and

(e)   determining the underlying causes including management-related causes.

269   You should outline your arrangements for ensuring that all the circumstances surrounding the failure, including human factors, are considered during the investigation. Your arrangements should be summarised under which corrective action is determined and taken. You also need to give a summary of the appropriate tracking carried out by management to confirm that the necessary work is completed properly.

Review and audit

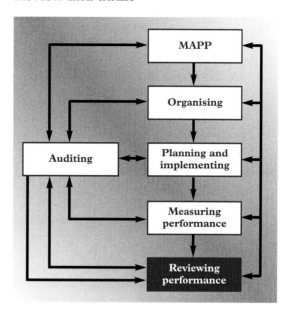

Review

270   Review is an essential process for determining if the SMS is appropriate to fulfil the MAPP and the objectives set within it. It may involve considering whether the MAPP and objectives should themselves be modified. Review is necessary for determining required improvements to management systems, physical controls or the MAPP itself.

271   Your safety report should show that your company has adopted and implemented a review process which uses information from performance measurement and audit. You should include, for example:

(a)   summaries of your company's arrangements for carrying out reviews, explaining who does them, and when and how they are conducted;

(b)   reference to the arrangements under which the results of investigation of substandard performance - from active and reactive performance measurement - are analysed in a systematic way so that common problems, features and trends are determined and that this information is used to inform decisions;

(c)   summaries of your company's arrangements for deciding whether corrective or improvement action is required, and for allocating responsibilities for carrying it out; and

(d) outlines of the mechanisms for setting timescales for the completion of remedial action, and for incorporating relevant remedial actions into improvement plans.

272 Your safety report should describe how the results of review are documented, as required by COMAH. You could include records of the results of recent reviews and descriptions of your arrangements for publishing the results within the organisation.

273 Your safety report should describe the arrangements by which the MAPP and SMS are updated by senior management. You should include, for example, summaries of the arrangements under which the MAPP and SMS are reviewed at board level or at the most senior management level.

274 You could refer to recent or current company improvement plans showing objectives aimed at updating or improving aspects of the SMS, such as training, active performance measurement, and incident investigation.

Audit

275 The term 'auditing' is often used to refer to activities such as safety tours, 'physical conditions' inspections, and behaviour observation carried out by line managers as part of their active performance monitoring activities. These are not the same as the audits mentioned in the COMAH Regulations. The former involve monitoring the outcomes of some aspects of the SMS whereas the latter involve fundamental assessment of the validity and reliability of the SMS itself.

276 Audits are needed to ensure that your organisation's processes and procedures, as defined and carried out in practice, are consistent with the SMS and that they are effective. Audits need to be carried out by people who are sufficiently independent of operational management to ensure that their assessment is objective.

277 Your safety report should show that your company has adopted and implemented a procedure for the systematic independent assessment of the MAPP and the effectiveness and suitability of the SMS. Under this you could include:

(a) descriptions of your arrangements for ensuring that the management arrangements, risk control systems and physical controls for the prevention and limitation of major accidents are assessed periodically by independent auditors;

(b) an explanation of the audit system which you have adopted - this might be a system which has been developed in- house or a proprietary system;

(c) an outline of the audit programme, defining:

(i) the purpose of the audits;

(ii) the responsibility for the audit programme as a whole, and for each audit within the programme;

(iii) the resources and personnel required for each audit, bearing in mind the need for expertise, operational independence and technical support;

(iv) the audit plan, indicating how it has been prioritised;

(v) the audit protocols to be adopted, which might include the use of questionnaires, checklists, and open and structured interviews, as well as checking documents, measurements and observations;

(vi) the procedures for reporting the audit findings;

(vii) the procedures for following up the recommendations shown to be necessary by audits; and

(viii) the procedures for reviewing the suitability and adequacy of the auditing arrangements themselves.

278   If it helps to show the extent of your audit approach, you could include an example of a recent audit report, including findings and recommended actions.

Information about possible major accidents

279   This chapter deals with the part of the safety report covering:

(a)   the description of the main activities at individual installations and the processes that go on there; and

(b)   the major accident hazards - how you identified them, the consequences and the risk analysis.

280   This information leads to the choice of measures, both engineering and procedural, to prevent and limit the consequences of a major accident, and the required information about these are dealt with in Chapter 6. Measures related to dealing with a major accident emergency are dealt with in Chapter 7.

Describing the processes, areas on site and scenarios that could lead to a major accident

Details about the processes which could lead to major accidents

281   You should describe the purpose of every installation which could give rise to a major accident. You should also describe:

(a)   the conditions under which the installation's dangerous substances are normally held;

(b)   what happens to the dangerous substances in terms of physical and chemical changes arising from the designed purpose of the plant;

(c)   what happens to the dangerous substances in terms of physical and chemical changes arising from foreseeable deviations from the designed purpose of the plant; and

(d)   the discharge, retention, reuse, recycling or disposal of residues, waste liquids and solids, and the discharge and treatment of waste gases;

where these are relevant to major accidents.

Details about the area on each installation which could lead to a major accident

282   For each installation, you should clearly identify, in overview, the location in terms of plant or activity, or both, where a major accident could happen. The safety report should:

(a)   include a plant diagram which clearly identifies key control and safety systems, reaction vessels, storage vessels, pipework systems, valves and significant connections; and

(b)   contain a plan which clearly identifies the location of activities where a major accident could happen, for example the storage of dangerous substances in packages or the processing of explosives.

Major accident scenarios

283   The major accident scenarios should include those initiated by or involving any of the dangerous substances on site, including those that do not form part of the qualifying inventory for a top-tier site requiring a safety report.

284   When writing a safety report, you must consider all accident scenarios involving a 'dangerous substance'. For an accident to be a 'major accident to the environment' (MATTE), it is not necessary for the 'dangerous substance' as defined by the Regulations to cause the impact, but merely to have played some part in the chain of events leading to a fire, explosion or major release.

285   For example, a major accident may be initiated by a 'dangerous substance', but another substance may cause the major accident and impact on the environment. This other substance may not be identified by COMAH but is present on the same site. In some circumstances, the substance which causes the impact may be something that appears relatively innocuous, eg glucose syrup or milk, but which could have a major impact on eco systems in releases to water.

286   For all dangerous substances, COMAH requires information as a minimum on hazard identification, and consequence analysis. The consequence analysis will help you in the preparation of your on-site emergency plan and provide information for the local authority in the preparation of the off-site emergency plan.

287   COMAH also requires a risk analysis (see glossary), for which the report should give information about the probabilities of the consequences described or should summarise the events which may play a role in triggering the scenarios. Whichever route is chosen, the report should include an assessment of the extent and severity of any possible major accident. If you decide to rely on a summary of the events that might trigger a major accident to support that assessment, you will have to treat the likelihood of each event as significant and satisfy yourself that the arguments presented in your safety report are consistent with the demonstrations required by the competent authority. This may well be practical for many installations where there are recognised standards or guidance, particularly when considering risks on site.

288   Your risk assessment determines whether the measures taken are all that are necessary. Risk assessment is fundamental to the demonstration. You need to decide the scope and nature of your risk assessment, so that it is fit for purpose in relation to the circumstances on your site and the demonstration required.

289   You are required to take necessary measures to prevent major accidents or limit their consequences, and to incorporate adequate safety and reliability of plant and equipment during its lifetime when linked to major hazards operations. The approach to selecting appropriate measures is discussed in paragraphs 340-349. For new or modified plant or installations, you should be able to demonstrate that you have looked at ways of avoiding hazards or reducing them at source by the application of principles of inherent safety. Even so, risks may still be significant for these plants and installations as well as existing installations. For these remaining risks, the demonstration that you have taken the necessary measures should be made on the basis of existing legal frameworks that risk should be reduced as low as reasonably practicable (ALARP) for health and safety matters, and the use of the best available techniques not entailing excessive costs (BATNEEC) for environmental matters.

290   A digest of the competent authorities' view on hazard, foreseeability and reasonable practicability can be found in Appendix 4.

291   This book will help you understand what steps you have to take to demonstrate that you have taken all the necessary measures to prevent major accidents or limit their consequences for the major hazards on site, including avoiding hazards at source, when that is reasonably practicable.

How much analysis do you have to do?

292   In broad terms, there is a range of risk assessment approaches of increasing complexity, from simple qualitative analyses through semi-quantitative analyses to fully quantified risk assessment (see Box A for definitions). The depth and type of your analyses will vary but is likely to be proportionate to:

(a)   the scale and nature of the major accident hazards presented by your establishment and the installations and activities on it;

(b)   the risks posed by your site to neighbouring populations and the environment, in other words the extent of possible damage; and

(c)   the complexity of the major accident hazard process and activities, and the difficulty in deciding and justifying the adequacy of the risk-control measures adopted.

Box A

(a) Qualitative risk assessment is the comprehensive identification and description of hazards from a specified activity, to people or the environment. The range of possible events may be represented by broad categories, with classification of the likelihood and consequences for comparison and the identification of priorities.

(b) Semi-quantitative risk assessment is the systematic identification and analysis of hazards from a specified activity, and their representation by means of qualitative and quantitative descriptions of the frequency and extent of the consequences, to people or the environment. The assessment is informed by a representative selection of specific examples for comparison with standards.

(c) Quantitative risk assessment is the application of methodology to produce a numerical representation of the frequency and extent of a specified level of exposure or harm, to specified people or the environment, from a specified activity. There is also a comparison of the results with specified criteria.

Examples

Example 1

A simple site
(such as a chlorine water treatment plant)
remote from population
(such as the Highlands of Scotland)
with a single dangerous substance
(say 30 te of chlorine)
presenting a limited range of hazards
(escape of a toxic gas)

may only require

a simple qualitative risk assessment (perhaps based on the HSE guidance HSG28 *Safety advice for bulk chlorine installations*[10] about the safe handling of chlorine, and the guidance published by the Chemical Industries Association (CIA) and the chlorine producers on emergency planning, with supporting

statements required to demonstrate that the risks to people and environment off site are ALARP) to demonstrate that the necessary prevention and limitation measures are in place, and limited quantification of the possible consequences to help develop the emergency plan.

Example 2

A complex site
(such as a chlorine production plant)
near to population and sensitive environments
(such as a town centre or SSSI)
with a number of dangerous substances
(say chlorine and ethyl chloride)
presenting an extensive range of hazards
(escape of toxic gases, flammable effects)

may require

a detailed assessment and some quantification of the likelihood of hazardous releases and their consequences, and possibly of the associated risks, to demonstrate that the necessary prevention and limitation measures are in place (to demonstrate that the risks to people and environment off site are ALARP), and quantification of the possible consequences to help develop the emergency plan.

Example 3

The off-site risks at an LPG facility* are often dominated by the fireball event scenario following whole tank failure, with the contribution from the vapour cloud explosion (VCE) scenario being much less significant. This means that the analysis of the drifting cloud scenario and possible VCE need not be comprehensive, but sufficient to show that the measures in place prevent or limit such scenarios.

Example 4

For explosives facilities and operations, a qualitative risk assessment approach based on the 'defence-in-depth' principle may be appropriate, unless the facility does not comply with 'quantity safety' distances. In this latter case, a quantified risk assessment is needed to demonstrate that all measures necessary to control the risks have been taken.

* Provided the vessels are not mounded or fitted with passive fire protection coatings.

> *Preparing information about major accident scenarios, including identifying all the possible major accidents, giving an estimate of how likely an accident may happen, and assessing the consequences of each possible accident*

Steps in preparing information about the major accident scenarios

293   There are three steps in preparing information about all major accident scenarios:

(a)   identify all the possible major accidents;

(b)   give a realistic estimate of the likelihood of each major accident hazard or an adequate summary of initiating events to support (a); and

(c)   produce an adequate assessment of the extent and severity of the consequences for each identified major accident hazard.

Step 1   Identify all the possible major accidents

294   To show that your risk analysis is comprehensive, your safety report should identify the full range of possible major accidents and describe a representative set of examples, sufficient to enable a comprehensive assessment of the consequences. If a possible major accident is identified, its consequences should be assessed.

295   For example, loss of a dangerous substance through failure of the pipework would be a potential major accident on many sites. There may be many different runs, sizes and types of pipework on site. You would not be expected to identify and analyse the major accident potential of every piece. However, a structured approach to hazard identification is required. You should analyse representative examples and apply the conclusions reached to the whole installation or even the site, if appropriate.

296   You should use, and describe in your safety report, a systematic process to identify all foreseeable major accidents. This is because the chemical industry is diverse and complex, and presents major accident hazards ranging from damage to water courses to toxic effects for people downwind of a warehouse fire. A structured approach to hazard identification is therefore required.

297   You should also consult the guidance given in documents *Guidance on the interpretation of a major accident to the environment for the purposes of the COMAH Regulations*[3] and also *Environmental risk assessment as regards COMAH.*[4]

> *Example 1*
>
> An operator of a manufacturing site is required to prepare a COMAH safety report because of the bulk storage of LPG. The site also has quantities of petroleum spirit (below the levels for notification as a lower-tier site). The consequences of a release of the latter should be considered by the operator and included in the safety report if such a release can cause a major accident.

> *Example 2*
>
> An operator stores bulk chlorine on site and therefore is required to prepare a safety report. The site also has quantities of flammable liquids well away from the chlorine storage. The report should consider pool fire hazards if such a fire itself can be a major accident or the consequences of such a fire can cause loss of containment of the chlorine, leading to a major accident.

298   Your identification process should cover the different types of major accident hazards, which can include:

(a)   loss of containment accidents due to vessel or pipework failures; these could lead to toxic releases, or for flammables which are ignited, to a range of fire and explosion hazards, eg fireballs, flash and jet fires and vapour cloud explosions (VCEs);

(b)   explosions, eg exothermic reactions in batch reactors and explosion due to operator error including the addition of the wrong materials;

(c) condensed phase explosions relating to explosives;

(d) large fires, for example in warehouses, and pool fires;

(e) events influenced by emergency action or adverse operating conditions. Examples include allowing a fire to burn rather than applying water, dumping reactor contents to drain to avoid explosion, and abnormal discharge to the environment; and

(f) other types of major accident hazard or abnormal discharge.

299 The major accident scenarios you present in the safety report should include the worst case scenarios (see glossary) and the most serious foreseeable events for people and the environment, taking into account what might happen on site as well as off site. A brief discussion on what is foreseeable can be found in Appendix 4.

300 One way of approaching this is to:

(a) identify the 'worst case scenarios' in relation to people and the environment; and

(b) assess the consequences - if they are trivial there is no need for further predictions, but if they are significant, a range of major accidents needs defining and analysing.

301 Methods of identification that many operators use include:

(a) HAZOP;

(b) safety reviews and studies of the causes of past major accidents and incidents;

(c) industry standards or bespoke checklists for hazard identification;

(d) failure mode and effects analysis (FMEA);

and specifically for dealing with human factors issues,

(e) job safety analysis, for example task analysis; and

(f) human error identification methods.

Step 2 Give a realistic estimate of the likelihood of each major accident hazard or an adequate summary of initiating events

302 Your safety report should either:

(a) contain estimates of the probability, in qualitative or quantitative terms, of each major accident scenario you have analysed; or

(b) set out the conditions under which the major accident scenarios could occur.

303 Whichever one you choose, you should include a summary of the initiating events and event sequences, internal or external, which may play a role in triggering each scenario.

304 If you use judgmental words to describe likelihoods such as 'likely' or 'non-credible', then the significance of these words should be clearly explained.

305 The safety report should explain the systematic process used to identify initiating events and subsequent event sequences including, where appropriate, information obtained from previous accidents and incidents, which can be a useful starting point.

306 The scope of such studies should consider the causes of accidents in other industries. You should show that the event sequences leading to the scenarios are correctly identified and justified.

307 When considering events that could lead to a major accident, you should think about whether a sequence or combination of events may lead to a major accident. If so, you should assess the effects of failure on systems, plant and equipment designed to prevent and detect such a scenario, and describe the measures taken to prevent this sequence occurring.

308   For automatic isolation systems, you should consider the situation where the system fails and the operator fails to respond correctly to an alarm. You should assess whether the severity of the hazard and the reliability of the automatic systems and human response are such that the risks remain ALARP.

309   Human error should be addressed by you as an accident initiating event, for example loading wrong reactants into a batch reactor, or a wrong operating procedure leading to an abnormal discharge to a water course.

310   You should clearly identify in the safety report all safety critical events and the associated initiators. Safety critical events are those that dominate the contribution to risk, so they should be identified by your risk analysis.

311   Safety critical events are key to identifying suitable control and protection measures for preventing hazardous events or limiting their consequences. However, the failure of these protection measures must also be considered in assessing whether the residual risks are ALARP or whether more needs to be done.

312   If you reject potential control measures, you should give reasons in the safety report. If you estimate, or make assumptions about the reliability of protective systems and the times for operators to respond and isolate loss of containment, then your estimates or assumptions should be realistic and adequately justified.

313   Qualitative arguments should be based on currently accepted good standards for engineering and safe systems of work. You should provide information in the safety report to support your view about the likely demand on the various control measures and systems, and what the consequences might be if these fail.

314   For example, if an operative has to intervene to close an isolation valve manually when automatic isolation fails, then the release duration will be determined by the time taken to intervene successfully. In such cases, release durations of less than 20 minutes will require justification.

315   Any methods you use to generate event sequences, and to estimate the probabilities of potential major accidents, should be appropriate and be used correctly.

316   This should include the use of:

(a)   relevant operational and historical data;

(b)   fault tree analysis (FTA);

(c)   event tree analysis (ETA); or

(d)   a combination of these.

317   The methods and assumptions you use should be described in the safety report. In particular, any failure rate data used for the base events in the FTA will need clear explanation in terms of the circumstances on your site.

318   It is not sufficient to adopt data from published sources without justifying their suitability to your site, unless you show that the conclusions of the risk analysis are not affected by such data. If they are sensitive to the data and assumptions used, suitable and sufficient justification is needed for their use.

319   The methods employed need to be fit for purpose and used correctly. You should describe the process and methods adopted to generate any probabilities or event sequences, together with assumptions and data sources used. Checks against company benchmarks must be included if you use them.

320   You need to assess the sensitivity of the conclusions to the assumptions and other uncertainties. For example, in the case of explosives facilities there is not much data on event probabilities, which causes uncertainty in the estimation process. The significance of this uncertainty should be discussed in your report.

321   If you use event probabilities which you know are not consistent with historical or relevant generic industry data, you should justify their use as it is likely to be challenged by the competent authority. For example, your justification may refer to quality procedures or plant experience.

Step 3 Produce an adequate assessment of the extent and severity of the consequences for each identified major accident hazard

322   Your safety report should provide details to show that the way you have assessed the consequences for each major accident scenario, with respect to people and the environment, is suitable and sufficient.

323   You should either describe or reference any consequence assessment model and methodology you have used. You should also justify the assumptions made and the values used in the key variables of the method or model, for example wind speed, atmospheric conditions and ground roughness in gas dispersion models.

324   The range of scenarios considered must be representative and suitable for emergency planning, which means that the consequences of catastrophic vessel failure and guillotine failure of pipework need to be included.

325   Different levels of harm need to be considered. As a minimum, you should consider how a major accident might affect people and the environment. Any impact criteria or vulnerability models you use, in predicting the extent of areas where people or the environment may be affected need to be defined and justified. For environmental impact assessment, the harms to consider should be short-term and long-term recoverable and non-recoverable destruction of plant life and fatality to animal life.

Information about the measures to prevent or limit the consequences of a major accident at each installation

326   This chapter deals with the part of the safety report which describes the measures provided for preventing or limiting the consequences of a major accident. Measures solely related to dealing with a major accident emergency are dealt with in Chapter 7.

327   The information in this chapter is closely linked to the information in Chapter 5, and is the part where you should describe and justify your choice of measures to prevent or limit the consequences of a major accident based on the major accident scenarios you have identified using the principles in Chapter 5. Equally, you need to show that there is adequate safety and reliability during the life cycle of your installation, equipment and infrastructure relevant to major accidents.

328   For large sites, with more than one installation, you could demonstrate that the necessary measures have been provided to prevent major accidents or limit their consequences as core information for the whole of the site. You could then refer to any differences to this general approach in the part of the report dealing with each installation (see paragraph 324).

329   Similarly, where there is more than one installation, you could describe the management of each installation and identify any differences in how the SMS has been put into effect at a particular installation to that described in the earlier part of the report. Overall, the measures you describe should show how the MAPP and SMS have been put into effect.

Describing the installation, plant and equipment in relation to how major accidents will be prevented or limited

Focused information to support the demonstration that major accident hazards will be prevented or limited

330   The safety report should include information about all the installations which have major accident potential. For each one,

there should be a description in enough detail to determine the purpose, location and function of equipment within the installation that has a bearing on major accident prevention and control.

331   The purpose of the information is to provide enough detail for assessors to understand your argument that you have taken the necessary steps to prevent a major accident or limit its consequences. So, you should provide a description focused on the demonstration being made, and at a level of detail sufficient for the assessors to understand the arguments presented.

332   Some information is best provided by drawings which are supported by description. The safety report should therefore contain plans, maps or diagrams plus descriptions which clearly set out detailed information about the installations with major accident potential. In particular, there should be information about items of plant where these are relevant to the major accident hazards on site, such as:

(a)   vessels, for example location, type, size, inventory, design and operating limits (eg temperatures and pressures), purpose and contents;

(b)   pipework systems containing dangerous substances, for example routes, types, size, design, flow rates and operating limits, and purpose;

(c)   services, for example steam, air, electricity, fuel and hot water;

(d)   drainage, for example routes and purpose (such as foul water and fire-fighting run-off water);

(e)   stacks, flares and gas cleaners, for example location and purpose;

(f)   safety- or environment-critical valves, instruments, control loops and detection systems;

(g)   fire-fighting and supply arrangements; and

(h) monitoring equipment, for example, for toxic products in air, sewers, discharges to water, and for fires or explosive atmospheres.

333 You should also include relevant information about:

(a) the normal operating parameters of the plant;

(b) the designed maximum working parameters, such as capacities, temperatures, pressures and maximum explosive inventories;

(c) relevant qualitative and quantitative information on energy and mass transport in the process (for example material and energy balances) during:

(i) normal running;

(ii) start-up or shutdown periods; and

(iii) abnormal operations;

(d) dangerous substance locations and, at each location, an indication of the chemical and physical state and quantity of the dangerous substance.

334 In providing your descriptions of the equipment and measures provided, you may decide to give information that is common to the site or common to the installation in one place and only deal with differences from these descriptions in the relevant parts of the report dealing with the installation. An example of this approach might be your description of how you decide what overpressure protection to provide on vessels. You may have a policy of providing protection to prevent rupture of vessels as a result of fire engulfment, which you could justify once and not repeat in the report. You then only need to identify, say, those vessels protected by pressure relief valves to prevent overpressure from other causes, such as exothermic reactions and process excursion.

> *Describing how the measures taken will prevent or limit the consequences of a major accident. Measures can be categorised into four levels: inherent safety; prevention measures; control measures; limitation measures*

Show how the measures taken prevent or limit the consequences of major accidents

335 This is a fundamental demonstration. Your safety report should demonstrate how the measures taken will prevent foreseeable failures which could lead to the major accidents that you have identified. It should show how each measure contributes to the defence against each hazardous event. Where representative events have been chosen, the measures for preventing or limiting a major accident can relate to a broad range of events with similar outcomes.

336 In your safety report, you should show how your approach will be applied to new and modified facilities that are being installed, and what procedures there are for applying the approach when designing new plants or modifications to existing ones. You need to describe how you set priorities for deciding which measures to take. The following section gives advice on how the competent authority judges the priorities should be set, and presents them in a hierarchy.

337 Your safety report should also demonstrate how adequate safety and reliability have been built into the measures for preventing or limiting the consequences of a major accident during the full life cycle of each installation. This is also a very important demonstration and is discussed later in this chapter (see paragraph 350).

338 For existing establishments, the measures will already have been determined. In these cases, the competent authority will not be so much concerned about how the measures were selected in the past but more in a description of what they are and what they aim to do. The competent authority will want to know that the measures selected and used together have the necessary safety and reliability to prevent major accidents or limit their consequences.

339 The measures may take the form of hardware, software systems or human factors. It is important that the performance specified for the risk-reduction measures should be related to realistic scenarios. Guidance on the range of measures to be applied and the issues to be considered in their selection are outlined in the following paragraphs.

Selection of measures

340 The initial design stage presents the best opportunity to remove hazards and reduce risk. This opportunity can also be taken in the design of modifications. This means that operators of older establishments should be alert to technical advances in their industry to improve safety.

341 Your approach to the selection of measures should set priorities for making decisions on the measures to use. You will have procedures that deal with new or modified installations, however the competent authority will be looking for an approach which reflects the following four levels in a hierarchy.

Level 1: inherent safety

342 Inherent safety is concerned with the removal or reduction of a hazard at source.

343 Examples of inherently safe techniques include:

(a)   substitution of a less hazardous process;

(b)   use of corrosion-resistant materials of construction;

(c)   reduction or elimination of hazardous inventory;

(d)   design for maximum foreseeable operating conditions; and

(e)   fail-safe design principles and appropriate plant layout.

344 It is very unlikely that, whichever design is chosen, the installation will be without any risk and so many people refer to this as the inherently safer approach. However, the focus of the approach is still to remove or reduce hazard at source.

Level 2: prevention measures

345 These are intended to prevent the initiation of a sequence of events which could lead to a major accident. They can:

(a)   be management systems or features of the design of the installation;

(b)   be applied during design, construction, operation, maintenance and modification;

(c)   be designed to prevent failure of equipment or human error and include individual activities, for example maintenance or inspection, aimed at preventing specific failures; and

(d)   include hardware arrangements such as double-walled piping to provide a secondary containment, or use of canned or magnetic drive pumps.

Level 3: control measures

346 These are intended to prevent a hazardous event from escalating into a major accident. They include measures directed at preventing or limiting small releases which have the potential to escalate to a major accident. Examples of control measures include:

(a)   relief valves;

(b)   safety-related control systems;

(c)   deluge systems;

(d)   venting to scrubbing systems or flare stacks;

(e)   manually initiated emergency shutdown procedures; and

(f)   gas detection systems.

347 Control measures should be independent from the cause of the initiating hazardous event and associated systems, so as not to fail as a direct result of the event.

Level 4: limitation measures

348   These are measures which are taken to reduce the consequences of a major accident once it has occurred. Examples of these include:

(a)   safety refuges;

(b)   bunding systems to protect surface and groundwaters, and underground drains to protect groundwaters;

(c)   fire-fighting facilities;

(d)   emergency response procedures; and

(e)   traverses or mounds for explosives buildings.

349   Chapter 7 of this book gives more detail on limitation measures relating to emergency response.

> *Describing how adequate safety and reliability have been built into the installation. There are five main elements to consider, relating to the life cycle of the installation*

How to show that adequate safety and reliability have been built into the installation to prevent or limit the consequences of major accidents

350   When demonstrating that adequate safety and reliability have been built into the installation, there are four main elements referred to in Schedule 4 Part 1. A fifth element, modification, is often more easily described as a separate element. The four main elements are:

(a)   design - includes plant layout, process design and design of equipment; discussion of conceptual design is very important for new or modified installations;

(b)   construction - includes the manufacture, installation, construction of civil structures, testing, initial inspection and commissioning;

(c)   operation - includes plant start-up, shutdown, normal operation, including foreseeable temporary operations, emergency shutdown and the extent to which deviation from normal operation will be tolerated;

(d)   maintenance - includes preventive maintenance, repair, replacement, periodic examination by a competent person, and the assessment of any defects found; and

the additional element is:

(e)   modification - includes the measures to deal with changes that may take place on the installation during its life, including all alterations, and during decommissioning, which could affect the integrity of the remaining installation.

(a) Adequate safety and reliability in design

351   Your aim should be to show in your safety report that the establishment and installations have been designed to an appropriate standard. This is essential for reports on new or modified plant. Full information is also more likely to be available for more recently constructed plant. However you must be able to establish the operating limits for all your plant. For older plant in particular, the safety report should make it clear what additional (if any) systems or arrangements are in place to prevent or limit a major accident to take account of plant built to standards that have since been superseded or that have been introduced as a result of long operational experience on site.

352   You should give a clear description of your approach to the selection of measures as part of your system for designing plant. Any design standard should also have addressed the following **ten key issues**, and your safety report should highlight these.

Key issues in design

1 redundancy, diversity, separation and segregation;

2 impact of a single event which may have multiple effects;

3 layout of the plant;

4 reliability, availability and survivability of utilities;

5 containment;

6 structural integrity, including:

    (a) design codes or standards;

    (b) evidence of conformity;

    (c) normal operation and foreseeable extremes; and

    (d) materials of construction;

7 protection from excursions beyond design condition, including;

    (a) normal operating limits; and

    (b) safe operating limits;

8 safety-related control systems;

9 human factors; and

10 systems for identifying locations where flammable substances could be present.

Design key issue 1: redundancy, diversity, separation and segregation

353   You should show in your safety report how the principles of redundancy, diversity, separation and segregation have been applied to reduce the risk of common-mode or common-cause failure and to ensure the availability of support systems, for example a battery back-up to an essential power supply.

354   You should also address the behaviour of equipment on failure, and include events which may cause a fault and disable protective systems.

Design key issue 2: impact of a single event which may have multiple effects

355   Where a single event, such as the loss of power supply, can affect some or all parts of an establishment at once, then the risk of it leading to a major accident are much increased. Your safety report should show that the cumulative effects of such an event have been considered. This includes events that are internal to the installation such as power failure, and external events such as flooding or an earthquake.

Design key issue 3: layout of the plant

356   The layout of the plant should limit the risk during operations, inspection, testing, maintenance, modification, repair and replacement.

357   The design of plant layout can make a big contribution to reducing the likelihood and consequences of a major accident. Your safety report should show that due attention has been given to ensuring safety in the design of the layout of the installation. In particular, it should show how the layout prevents or reduces the development of major accident scenarios. Examples of how this might be achieved include the following:

(a)   adequate ventilation to aid rapid dilution of flammable atmospheres;

(b)   low congestion of structures, equipment, plant or any other obstacle to gas flow that could aggravate the pressure effects resulting from the ignition of a release of a flammable substance;

(c)   separation of known sources of fire risk from large potential inventories, for example pumps which may leak, spark or overheat have often been located under overhead pipe racks;

(d)   adequate shelter for use during any toxic release and adequate means of escape during other emergencies;

(e)   access for emergency services;

(f)   access for inspection, testing, maintenance and repair, at all times throughout the life of the plant;

(g) separation of hazardous plant from the site boundary to reduce off-site risk, and to reduce risk to the plant from off-site causes such as fires;

(h) safe positioning of occupied buildings;

(i) separation of hazardous plant from structures whose own failure constitutes a hazard to the plant; and

(j) ease of access for decontamination of explosives plant and equipment.

Examples

The explosives industry provides a particular case of the use of layout to ensure safety. At licensed explosives sites, appropriate distances related to the quantities of explosives are maintained between explosives holdings, to limit the consequences of any explosion. For example, magazines are separated from each other so that in the event of an incident in one magazine, the explosives in the adjacent magazines are not affected. Larger distances are also used to protect people both on and off site.

Certain explosives manufacturing operations carry such a likelihood of accidental initiation with unacceptable consequences that they are performed remotely, for example in earth-mounded concrete cells, with operators in a safe control room. Other process operations with potential high frequency but small hazards are conducted behind protective screens or barricades, such as a polycarbonate safety screen if the quantity of explosives is small enough.

Design key issue 4: reliability, availability and survivability of utilities

358 Utilities that are needed to implement any measure defined in the safety report should have the necessary reliability, availability and survivability to prevent or limit the consequences of a major accident.

359 Failure of a utility, for example water, air, steam or electricity (including power surge or partial loss), often results in a process upset, and may have effects across the entire establishment. Failure of an emergency facility, for example firewater, has the potential to cause a relatively small incident to escalate into a major accident. Your safety report should justify the steps that have been taken in design, including for construction, operation and maintenance, to ensure that these utilities and facilities will be available when and for as long as is required.

360 The justification that the utilities are suitable may include reference to:

(a) the routing of services;

(b) physical protection, for example barriers and insulation;

(c) the provision of separate independent sources;

(d) the segregation of duplicated supplies;

(e) the means of managing changed demands, for example during start-up and shutdown, and abnormal operation; and

(f) the methodology adopted to allow continued availability of essential services while allowing maintenance activities or modifications to be carried out safely.

Design key issue 5: containment

361 Your safety report should identify the means by which dangerous substances can be accidentally released from the containment, and the measures provided to prevent that. It should also demonstrate the suitability of the measures to prevent releases. Such measures may include:

(a) control measures used in the design to reduce potential sources of release which include, for example, the location, number and type of joints. Any joints used should be suitable for the intended purpose considering the nature of the contained material, operating conditions and the degree of danger this represents;

(b) design requirements for temporary arrangements, taking into account possible movement, for example flexible connections between fixed storage or piping systems and mobile tankers or vessels;

(c)   location of vessels and equipment, and routing of pipework, to reduce the risk of a major accident;

(d)   maintenance and inspection requirements addressed at the design stage; and

(e)   process design and control for exothermic reactions.

362   With certain exceptions, such as explosives where confinement may increase the hazard, dangerous substances provide less of a hazard if they are contained within the plant. This is particularly so of hazards to the environment. You should show in your safety report how your establishment has been designed with this in mind.

363   Your safety report should include details of systems designed to control loss of containment and to manage unplanned releases. These could include:

(a)   *venting systems* - your safety report should justify the design basis for any venting system, taking into account foreseeable hazards, including the loss of utilities or the effects of fire, and the consequences of venting to the environment.

(b)   *isolation arrangements* - your safety report should describe and justify the emergency automatic and manual isolation arrangements to manage a release, including consideration of the time required to isolate. If you have a company standard, give details and reference to this should be adequate unless there are any deviations from it, which should then be justified. Appropriate performance standards for emergency isolation should be stated and justified in the safety report.

(NB Isolation may also be necessary for maintenance, but the arrangements for this will be different from those required for emergency isolation where speed of response and accessibility may be important.)

(c)   *other prevention and containment systems* - your safety report should justify the design basis for each of these measures taking into account the foreseeable hazards.

(NB In the case of some situations involving explosives, it may be more appropriate to limit the effects of an explosion through reducing the containment or confinement of the explosive.)

(d)   *detection of releases* - in the event of a loss of containment, measures should be provided to limit the risk arising. This may involve further containment or control of the material, or both, or help for dispersal. Where the potential for loss of containment of a significant quantity of dangerous substances can be foreseen, measures to limit the consequences should be taken, for example bunding, catchment pits, dump tanks, diversion walls or grading of the ground.

364   Your safety report should identify such measures and demonstrate the adequacy of the design, including consideration of the maximum expected spill.

365   All foreseeable direct causes of loss of containment accidents should be considered at the design stage. The majority of direct causes fall into one of the following categories. Your safety report should show that these causes have been considered and suitable measures taken:

(a)   *corrosion* - may be internal or external, and may be enhanced by synergistic effects such as stress-corrosion cracking or erosion-corrosion. The safety report should identify particular areas where corrosion may occur and the measures taken to prevent and monitor such effects, for example design codes, construction standards, protective systems (inert linings, cathodic protection etc) and periodic inspection.

(b) *erosion* - may be caused by excessive fluid velocity, a change in phase, cavitation or the presence of particulates. Your safety report should identify particular areas where erosion may occur and the measures taken to prevent and monitor such effects, including periodic inspection.

(c) *external loading* - may be caused by extreme weather or ground movement (seismicity), by the forces applied during construction or during operation, and by failures of pipe or vessel supports nearby. Your safety report should show that the foreseeable events will not affect the integrity of the containment or its supporting structure.

(d) *impact* - damage may occur from road and rail vehicles, or from missiles from failed equipment and other sources. The blast wave from an incident on a nearby plant may also cause impact damage. Your safety report should identify the main sources of impact considered in the design and the critical items of plant exposed to impact damage. It should also show that adequate precautions have been put into effect.

(e) *pressure* - over- or under-pressure may cause loss of containment. Your safety report should show how excess pressure will be prevented during foreseeable failures, such as the failure of:

   (i) process controls between the system and other higher pressure systems or sources;

   (ii) over-pressure safety devices;

   (iii) external fire;

   (iv) internal explosion;

   (v) excessive reaction rate; and

   (vi) liquid expansion or exothermic reaction causing an increase in temperature and pressure.

The safety report should also cover vacuum, if it has been identified as a hazard condition.

(f) *temperature* - excessively high or low temperatures of the containment structure may reduce its strength or make it susceptible to brittle failure. Excessively high rates of change in temperature may also generate high thermal stresses. Your safety report should identify the precautions in place to prevent thermal problems due to process upsets, fire, or possibly adverse weather conditions in the case of plant exposed to the elements. Examples of precautions taken may include separation, water deluge, insulation, fire walls, heat tracing or other suitable means.

(g) *vibration* - may be generated within the containment, caused by changes in phase, water hammer, high pressure drop or cavitation. Externally generated vibration may be due to the incorrect positioning of pumps, poor piping design, etc. Excessive vibration may induce fatigue failure of the containment. Your safety report should show how vibration has been assessed, and any potential problems addressed.

(h) *wrong equipment* - if the wrong equipment has been specified or installed, there is a potential for failure. The safety report should identify the management controls in place to ensure correct specification, supply and installation of equipment, including spare parts.

(i) *defective equipment* - may cause failure due to pre-existing flaws, high stress, etc. Your safety report should show that suitable management procedures are in place to identify faults and control or limit effects of failure.

(j) *human error* - human error may cause failure of the containment by overfilling or overloading, or by some other manually initiated maloperation, for example operator initiates valve opening, and includes failure to take the required action. The safety report should consider the possibility and effects of human error and describe the measures in place to minimise the risk.

Design key issue 6: structural integrity

366   There are four elements to this key issue:

(a)   design codes or standards;

(b)   evidence of conformity;

(c)   normal operation and foreseeable extremes; and

(d)   materials of construction.

Design codes or standards

367   Your safety report should show how structures important to safety have been designed to provide adequate integrity.

368   You should provide sufficient evidence to show that the design of all structures important to safety has been based on sound engineering principles. This includes process and storage vessels, pipework and other items which achieve the primary containment.

369   Other key structural items, such as support structures, bund walls, civil foundations, control rooms, buildings or barriers designed to withstand the effects of accidental explosions, should also be included where they are important to your demonstration.

370   You should refer to any relevant design codes or standards which have been used. Reference to recognised standards, eg BS 5500, is normally sufficient as long as the plant is operating within the parameters set by the standards. Where used, design standards or codes should have been fully applied. If not, you should explain why you think that the design is appropriate and within the scope of the standards used. The competent authority will look carefully at your demonstration where you combine different design codes or standards to make your arguments. You should include information about any non-conformity with standards used.

371   Deviations from the principal design codes used, or features not within the standard design type, should be highlighted and described in the safety report. They warrant special attention, as should any features not within the standard design type. If a relevant design standard or code has not been used, your safety report should provide a justification for, and description of, the design method adopted.

Evidence of conformity

372   Your safety report should confirm that the design of structures important to safety is supported by any necessary documentation, to give an assurance of conformity. Compliance with design standards and codes establishes a baseline for the structural integrity of plant.

Normal operation and foreseeable extremes

373   The safety report should provide details of the normal operating conditions of the plant and any foreseen operational extremes.

374   Your safety report should show how the containment structure has been designed to withstand the loads experienced during normal operation of the plant and all foreseeable operational extremes during its expected life.

375   Information presented in the safety report should therefore show that it has taken account of all the conditions that the containment must withstand, such as external loads, ambient temperatures and the full range of process variations, for example normal operation, start-up and shutdown, turndown, regeneration, process upset, emergencies and explosions.

376   Your safety report should show that structures, components, pressurised equipment and systems will perform their required safety functions throughout their total life, under all foreseeable operational and fault conditions. The demonstration should consider the various loading conditions arising, and show how the effects of any degradation processes on the integrity of the containment have been catered for in the design, for example corrosion allowance approach.

377   Your safety report should provide an outline of the approach applied to the setting of design margins over maximum expected

operating conditions, such that the safe working limits of the plant, pressures, temperatures, flow rates, etc, are compatible with all expected operating extremes.

378   Specific details should be given where actual applied margins differ significantly from the approach normally applied or industry practice. The safety implications arising from the variation should be described and justified.

379   In some cases, such as with propellants and pyrotechnics, the containment should be designed to afford as little confinement as possible. In such instances, the safety report should justify the design approach of the containment structures and show that they will perform their required safety functions.

Materials of construction

380   Your safety report should show that construction materials used in the plant are suitable for the application. It should provide evidence that:

(a)   all materials employed in the manufacture and construction of the plant are suitable; particular attention should be given to the selection of materials used for the primary containment of hazardous substances;

(b)   materials have been selected with regard to the nature of the environment in which they will be used, for example the substances being handled, process conditions such as temperature, pressure and flow, possible sources of corrosion, and erosion;

(c)   the external environment, such as the effects of sea air in coastal areas, has been considered; and

(d)   the effects of impurities on the containment materials have been allowed for. (Impurities are regarded as including unwanted by-products of reaction as well as imported impurities.) The evidence should consider the impurities likely to be present under normal operating conditions and those that could foreseeably be present due to abnormal conditions, such as process upset or maloperation.

381   If a design code or standard has been used which includes materials selection criteria, any deviation from the materials specified in the code should be justified in the safety report.

382   Where materials selection is critical to safety, the safety report should include a description of the materials selection approach, for example where:

(a)   vessels will be used at very low temperature;

(b)   materials are required to contain particularly aggressive or corrosive substances;

(c)   materials will be used with explosives; or

(d)   a novel or unusual use of materials is proposed.

383   In such cases, your safety report should show that alternative materials were considered and assessed before the final selection was made.

Design key issue 7: protection from excursions beyond design conditions

384   Your safety report should show that adequate safeguards have been provided to protect the plant against excursions beyond design conditions.

385   Typically, a plant is designed to operate within a given range of process variables: the normal operating limits. These are the operating constraints which apply to normal operating conditions. There are also the safe operating limits, which are the rated values on which the safety of the plant is based. An excursion beyond the safe operating limits may result in a significant risk of loss of containment, fire or explosion.

386   Safe operation depends on the measures to prevent excursions from occurring, for example safety-related control systems, relief systems, shutdown procedures, emergency vent and disposal systems.

387   Your safety report should contain a description of the approach underlying the application of these measures. It should

describe the foreseeable events that have been taken into account, drawing links between identified hazards, system integrity and the use of suitable standards or good industry practice. It should show how each measure has been designed, constructed and operated so they are available whenever the plant is operating.

Normal operating limits

388 Normal operating limits are set to ensure that a suitable margin is present between normal operating conditions and the safe operating limits. The margin should be set so that for foreseeable failures, for example equipment failure, appropriate corrective action can be taken before the safe operating limits are exceeded. The corrective action can be either automatic, manual, or a combination of both.

389 Control systems, manual and automatic, are the first line of defence against excursions beyond normal operating limits. However, the primary function of a control system is usually economic, ie it is intended to ensure that the plant operates efficiently and produces a product that is within specification.

390 Alarm systems usually detect excursions beyond normal operating limits, using sensors that may or may not be entirely independent of the control system. The operator is alerted, and then takes remedial action.

Safe operating limits

391 Safe operating limits are determined primarily by the process design and material specification, but are influenced by the age and condition of the plant and equipment. Where a control or alarm system has a role in the defence against excursions, beyond the safe operating limits, it should be assessed as a safety-related control system.

392 Your safety report should identify the shutdown procedures, and outline in principle how these work in conjunction with other measures to protect the plant against excursions beyond the safe operating limits. Reference should also be made to relevant operating manuals rather than providing

detailed descriptions. The shutdown procedure typically operates in conjunction with other measures such as:

(a) shutting off feed streams;

(b) shutting off heat sources;

(c) adding inhibitors to the reagent;

(d) flushing through of continuous processes;

(e) applying process cooling;

(f) operating vents; and

(g) shutting down equipment.

393 Pressure relief and emergency venting provide another protection against over-pressurisation of plant, and may be the last line of defence against failure and uncontrolled loss of containment.

Design key issue 8: safety-related control systems

394 Your safety report should describe the principles of how safety-related control systems have been designed to ensure safety and reliability. Reference could be made to relevant documents rather than provide detailed descriptions.

395 In this context, safety-related control systems include protective systems, eg emergency shutdown systems. Your report should show how the safety-related control systems will provide the required level of risk reduction, when related to the risk of a major accident and the reduction of risk achieved by other measures in place.

396 In your report, you should provide evidence to show that the complete system (from sensor to final element, including software and the human interface) has been considered. You should show how you have determined the required safety integrity levels for safety-related control systems, and you should show how you have met those requirements.

397 Your safety report should show how the required safety integrity has been achieved. This may include the use of accepted good practice, codes and standards, etc. It should also show the appropriate application of redundancy, diversity, separation and segregation to safeguard against the risks of common cause failure. This should include both hardware, software and human interfaces.

398 In your safety report, you should explain how the following have been identified and accounted for in the design of your safety-related control systems:

(a) safe operating limits and their relation to the set points for safety functions, including the selection of appropriate measurement instrumentation;

(b) the independence and separation from other systems or the initiating faults which require the operation of safety-related control systems. If the safety-related control systems are not separate from other equipment, the safety report should show that failures of connected equipment cannot affect the safety function. It should also show that single-point failures cannot result in the failure of both systems. If this is impossible, the connected equipment or system should be regarded as being part of the safety-related control system;

(c) operating conditions, including start-up and shutdown and unusual operating conditions, for example single train operation;

(d) operating duty, including shut-off requirements for valves and how their performance will be affected by the presence of corrosive or erosive conditions;

(e) inspection and maintenance requirements, including the provision of facilities for carrying out proof testing; and

(f) environmental considerations, including requirements to operate in flammable atmospheres, equipment which requires special environments, prevention and consideration of electromagnetic interference and weather.

399 Your safety report should identify and describe support systems and back-up measures for the control and protective systems, including their component parts, for example power supplies or pneumatic systems. Information should be presented to show that support systems and back-up measures have adequate safety and reliability.

Design key issue 9: human factors

400 The safety report should show how systems which require human interaction have been designed to take into account the needs of the user, and that they are reliable.

401 Your report should show how human factors have been accounted for in the design of equipment and in the operation, maintenance and modification of systems. Equipment or systems should be designed after consideration of how human errors can be reduced.

402 Human factors which are important to preventing and limiting major accidents, should be addressed within your safety report and include:

(a) ergonomics associated with the process-operating interface and the prevention of alarm floods;

(b) demonstration of the safety and reliability of any activities which rely primarily on human action; and

(c) competence of staff who perform key safety functions (see paragraphs 225-227).

403 Suitable evidence which you can present in the safety report may include, for example:

(a) consideration of how equipment design and the associated operating environment minimise human errors;

(b) a description of procedures for activities requiring human interaction;

(c) a description of training, including refresher training;

(d) a description of staffing levels and supervision;

(e) where a necessary measure relies on human intervention, an explanation as to why human intervention has been selected in preference to an automated system; and

(f) shift work and overtime arrangements to minimise fatigue.

Design key issue 10: systems for identifying locations where flammable substances could be present

404 Your safety report should describe the systems for identifying locations where flammable substances could be present, and describe how the equipment has been designed to take account of the risk.

405 You should explain how potentially hazardous (flammable and explosive atmosphere) areas have been identified and classified. This may have been through an area classification study in which those areas where a risk exists, owing to the normal, occasional or accidental release of process materials to atmosphere, have been designated in accordance with recognised standards.

406 Sources of ignition for flammable atmospheres may include electrical equipment, naked flames or hot surfaces, and static electrical discharge. Your safety report should indicate how the likely sources of ignition have been considered in the design, for example:

(a) electrical equipment selection for defined hazardous areas;

(b) avoidance of hot surfaces or naked flames, or sparks associated with equipment, such as through the use of spark arrestors; and

(c) control of static electrical build-up.

407 Radio-frequency radiation may cause an ignition hazard. The safety report should indicate whether there are strong radio transmitters in the vicinity, or whether the process includes devices which are particularly sensitive to radio-frequency radiation, for example the manufacture of explosive detonators.

408 Equipment selected for use in hazardous areas should be suitable for use in these areas under all foreseeable operating conditions, including normal operation, start-up, shutdown, emergency, cleaning, or any other expected condition throughout the life of the installation.

(b) Adequate safety and reliability in construction

409 Your safety report should show that the installations have been constructed to appropriate standards to prevent major accidents and limit the consequences.

410 You should show that construction of plant and associated equipment is managed to ensure that it is built in accordance with the design intent. This can form part of the description of your 'management of change procedures' discussed at paragraphs 255-256.

411 You should also show that the manufacture and construction of the plant has employed appropriate materials and construction methods, to minimise the occurrence of defects or damage which might affect plant integrity. Evidence should be provided by you to show that the construction work has been carried out by suitable personnel in accordance with appropriate procedures.

412 There should be a reference in your safety report to any relevant construction codes or standards which have been used. Where codes or standards have not been used or do not exist, you should provide evidence as to why you think that the procedures you have adopted are adequate.

413 The safety report should describe your arrangements for controlling and recording changes to the original design made during construction. Any deviations from the original that may affect safety should be identified, and the effect on safety demonstrated to be acceptable. Details should be provided where significant nonconformities in manufacture have been identified, or where substantial remedial work has been carried out.

414 Information in the safety report should show that the construction of the plant, including deviations from the original design, has been documented to give an assurance of conformity.

415 Your safety report should describe how the construction of all plant and systems is assessed and verified against the appropriate standards to ensure adequate safety. The information provided should show that the construction process has not compromised the design intent.

416 You should identify the key assessment and verification activities, and the stages at which they are undertaken. You should also provide an explanation of the methods used and show how they will ensure safety. The acceptance criteria for testing and examination programmes should be identified, where appropriate. Suitable information might include:

(a) how the required quality of work has been achieved;

(b) hydraulic pressure testing of containment structures, where this is a code requirement;

(c) examination of engineering structures using appropriate non-destructive testing techniques;

(d) leak testing to confirm the capability of containment to prevent liquid or gaseous leakage;

(e) the mechanisms used to confirm the safety of all the elements of control systems, including valves, instruments, software, trips and alarms;

(f) the role and competence of any inspection authority employed to verify compliance with code requirements; and

(g) a reference to relevant quality assurance procedures.

417 You should provide information to show that commissioning trials have been conducted to confirm the safety provisions relating to plant design, operating limits and predicted performance, particularly the safety provisions.

(c) Adequate safety and reliability during operation

418 The safety report should show that safe operating procedures have been established and are documented for all reasonably foreseeable conditions, including start-up, shutdown and abnormal operating conditions, and in particular for safety critical purposes.

419 The safety report should identify how reviews of operating procedures are undertaken and recorded, to take account of operational experience or changing conditions in the plant. Paragraphs 270-274 provide more details on this.

420 During the operational life of the plant there may be temporary constraints in force, for example the use of overrides and procedures covering abnormal operation, or covering start-up and shutdown. Your safety report should show how these operational constraints are applied and managed, to ensure safety.

421 Information you provide about your management systems (see Chapter 4) will be relevant to show that adequate safety and reliability have been built into the operation of the installation. However, remember, if there are any installation-specific management systems to ensure safety, your safety report should give details.

(d) Adequate safety and reliability involving maintenance

422 Your safety report should show that an appropriate maintenance scheme is established for plant and systems, to prevent major accidents or limit their consequences.

423 You should show in your safety report that the maintenance procedures are sufficiently comprehensive to maintain the plant and equipment in a safe state. You should also show that maintenance activities will not compromise the safety of the installation and that maintenance staff will not be exposed to unacceptable risks.

424 Your safety report should describe the organisation of maintenance activities. The general principles of control, competence, co-operation and communication which should be demonstrated are outlined in paragraph 213 and the following paragraphs. For maintenance systems, assessors will look for information about:

(a)   fault reporting systems;

(b)   the availability and deployment of suitable personnel and equipment; and

(c)   the scheduling and ranking of routine maintenance activities.

425 The safety report should identify those plant items and systems for which maintenance is considered to be a safety critical activity. Evidence should be provided to justify the maintenance strategy adopted - see the section on major accident scenarios, paragraphs 283-291. The information you present may include:

(a)   arrangements for the periodic inspection and calibration of pressure relief devices;

(b)   the monitoring of internal corrosion, where this is a life-limiting feature;

(c)   the maintenance of utilities systems, for example electricity distribution, or ancillary equipment, for example pumps, where failure may lead directly to a hazardous situation;

(d)   the provision of installed spare equipment or spares in stock, where extended plant or system downtime could affect safety;

(e)   arrangements for the proof testing of all safety-related control system elements, for example sensors, transmitters, actuators, alarms, trips, and confirmation of software modification number. This is to reveal any faults which are not apparent during normal operation;

(f)   arrangements for the maintenance of control and instrumentation systems; and

(g)   inspection and maintenance of electrical earthing and lightning protection systems, particularly in a hazardous environment, for example explosives manufacture.

426 Your safety report should show that the impact of maintenance work on the safety of the installation has been adequately considered. Suitable evidence may describe, for example:

(a)   measures taken to ensure that the isolation of vessels will not compromise pressure relief systems;

(b)   the use of overrides in safety systems; and

(c)   relevant systems of work.

427 Your safety report should show that procedures and equipment are in place to ensure that plant is made safe before starting maintenance work and for the reinstatement of plant to the operating state after maintenance is properly managed. Appropriate information may include:

(a)   a description of the types of permit-to-work system in use;

(b)   procedures and equipment used for the release of pressure, draining, isolation, purging and ventilating of plant, and the removal of temporary isolation following maintenance; and

(c)   auditing arrangements to ensure that the permit-to-work system is being properly used.

428 The information should include, where appropriate, reference to any maintenance records kept, or other relevant documentation. In the case of pressure systems, the safety report should provide evidence that maintenance has been carried out in accordance with the Pressure Systems and Transportable Gas Container Regulations, regulation 12, and that records under regulation 13 have been kept.

Hazardous conditions

429   Your safety report should identify the procedures that are necessary to enable maintenance activities to be carried out safely to prevent a major accident. Safe systems of work should have been established to enable all activities which could result in dangerous situations to be identified. The information you provide may refer to:

(a)   hazards posed by electrical equipment and the procedures for making safe;

(b)   hazards associated with hot work, and procedures for assessing the risk or testing for flammable gases; and

(c)   hazards associated with underground services, and procedures for keeping contractors informed about such services in the area where they are working.

430   Your safety report should identify which activities are subject to a permit-to-work system and describe the key features of the systems in use on your establishment. Suitable evidence should show how controls and limitations are placed on the maintenance activity, such as safe-working procedures, location of work, type of work, extent of work, competence of personnel, and time.

431   The safety report should show how all personnel, including contractors, involved in maintenance activities are made aware of the conditions and limitations of the permit-to-work system.

432   Where equipment has been certified by a third party, for example suitable for use in a flammable atmosphere, the safety report should justify how the maintenance system ensures the level of safety of that equipment. For instance this can be done by maintaining to standards in accordance with manufacturers' instructions.

Plant inspection

433   Your safety report should show that systems are in place to ensure that safety critical plant and systems are examined at appropriate intervals by a competent person.

434   Examinations by a competent person at intervals may be necessary because certain specialised skills or equipment are required, or because it is demanded by specific legislation, for example the Pressure Systems and Transportable Gas Container Regulations.

435   Your safety report should provide information to show that any competent person you employ has the necessary skills, knowledge and degree of independence from the production activity. The information you provide should also outline the arrangements for managing the activities of a competent person, who may be from a third-party or in-house organisation.

436   Your safety report should describe how the plant and systems which are subject to examination by a competent person are selected, and the reasons for the selection.

437   You should outline and justify the interval between examination by a competent person for the various types of safety critical plant and systems. You should identify, in general terms, the examination techniques which are employed and provide suitable justification for their selection. You should also explain how examinations by a competent person are properly planned and considered.

438   Your safety report should identify any safety critical plant or systems which are known to be susceptible to defects, which have been repaired, or where there is a history of failures. In such cases, evidence should be presented to show adequate monitoring of the situation and to provide details of any replacement programme.

439   The safety report should describe and justify the arrangements for reporting, recording and acting on the results of examinations by a competent person. For example, in the case of pressure systems, the safety report should provide evidence that they have been examined in accordance with the written scheme under regulation 9 of the Pressure Systems and Transportable Gas Container Regulations.

440   In the case of electrical equipment, there should be evidence of examination arrangements for equipment provided for use in hazardous areas.

441 Your safety report should show that there is a system in place to ensure the continued safety of the installations based on the results of periodic examinations and maintenance. You should describe how defects detected during maintenance or examination are properly assessed by a competent person to determine their significance and appropriate action taken. In summary, appropriate information in the safety report should include:

(a) management responsibilities for ensuring that defects are assessed and that any necessary corrective action is taken;

(b) the use of suitable assessment procedures, including references to published or company guidelines used to set defect acceptance levels; and

(c) the competence of any person carrying out the assessment of defects, and undertaking any associated corrective action.

(e) Adequate safety and reliability involving modification

442 Decommissioning of facilities is included under this heading.

443 Your safety report should describe the systems in place for ensuring that modifications are adequately conceived, designed, installed and tested.

444 Management systems for change are described in detail in paragraphs 255-256. Modifications to processes and associated equipment, and structures (including warehouses), or to operations and procedures, which could affect the safety of the installation should normally be subject to a formal modification system. This should cover both hardware measures, for example pumps, piping arrangements and structures, and software measures, for example control system software and operating systems.

445 Where arrangements exist for temporary modifications, they should be identified in the safety report, together with procedures for reinstatement as appropriate. Your safety report should identify how risk is assessed and decisions are made on temporary modifications.

446 The assessment and control over the modification process should remain to the same standard for temporary arrangements. Indeed, they may require higher scrutiny where the nature of temporary plant is inherently less safe than permanent arrangements, for example the use of flexible hoses or connections, or 'site-run' piping in place of permanent fully designed hard-piped systems.

447 Throughout the lifetime of an installation, there may be occasions requiring the decommissioning and removal of plant or components, for example as part of a modification programme or as part of risk reduction through the removal of redundant plant.

448 Your safety report should identify significant decommissioned plant and its relationship to the remaining related plant and systems. Removal of such plant should not lead to an increased risk associated with the use of the remaining plant and systems.

449 Particular care should be given to ensuring the integrity of remaining related safety systems following the removal of plant, and such arrangements should be included in the description of your change system. For example, this might include ensuring that:

(a) sections of fire protection systems, such as deluge supplies to a pressure vessel, are not compromised by physical isolation following the removal of redundant sections of the firewater supply system;

(b) shutdown systems are not compromised through computer software logic changes; and

(c) levels of equipment protection have not been reduced through the decommissioning of selected instrumentation or utility services, etc.

Information about the emergency response measures to limit the consequences of major accidents

450   This chapter covers the information you should give in your safety report about the range of emergency measures which you have in place to respond to major accident hazards. These include resources which can be mobilised such as fire-fighting equipment, and the provision for restoration and clean up.

451   The detailed operation of your emergency response measures will be included in your on-site emergency plan. Guidance on preparing this plan can be found in HSG191 *Emergency planning for major accidents.*[2] There is no need to include your plan with your safety report, indeed the competent authority would prefer that you did not. However your safety report should give information about key points including the minimum information required by Schedule 4 Part 2 (see Appendix 1).

452   If you do submit your on-site emergency plan, the report should clearly indicate where the key points outlined in this chapter can be found, supported by your arguments as to why you think that you have taken the measures necessary to limit the consequences of a major accident.

453   Your aim should be to demonstrate that you have taken the measures necessary to limit the consequences of a major accident, and that you have drawn up an on-site emergency plan to take these into account. Your measures should be related, and preferably cross-referenced, to the major accident scenarios described elsewhere in your safety report.

454   During the transition period for the implementation of COMAH, your report may have to be submitted before your COMAH on-site emergency plan has to be completed. In this case, you should describe the principles on which you will be building your plan, drawing on the principles of your existing emergency arrangements as appropriate.

455   Chapter 4 deals with risk control systems. The organisation of the alert and intervention in an emergency forms part of your safety management system and could follow the management model described there. It is described in this chapter to provide a complete picture on emergency response.

456   This chapter also deals with mobilisable resources, ie human resources and equipment, but not engineering measures relating to installations, which is dealt with generally in Chapter 6. However, you may like to deal with these issues together in your report.

Elements necessary to draw up the on-site emergency plan

457   Your safety report should summarise the measures of protection and intervention which have been used as the basis for drawing up the on-site emergency plan.

458   Your summary should cover:

(a)   the equipment installed in the plant to limit the consequences of a major accident;

(b)   the organisation of the alert and intervention; and

(c)   the on-site and off-site resources that may be mobilised.

(a) Equipment installed on plant to limit the consequences of a major accident

459   You will need to refer to fixed equipment installed on plant that limits the consequences of a major accident and how this equipment affects how an emergency is handled, for example emergency shutdown arrangements, including the extent of manual interaction required. A description of such equipment and its design and maintenance will generally be included with the information described in Chapter 6.

(b) Organisation for alerting and intervening in the case of an emergency

460   Your safety report should describe the organisation of the alert and intervention in the event of a major accident. The description could include the following, if they are relevant to the major accident scenarios on your site:

(a)   the functions of key posts and groups with duties in the emergency response and the arrangements for deputies, for example:

    (i)   the posts authorised to set the emergency procedures in motion and the conditions for doing so;

    (ii)   the post responsible for the co-ordination of the on-site limitation action;

    (iii)   the post responsible for liaising with the off-site emergency services; and

    (iv)   the role of any specialist groups required under the on-site emergency plans;

(b)   the arrangements for controlling and limiting the escalation of accidents on site, including:

    (i)   the isolation of hazardous inventories and the removal of inventories, where appropriate;

    (ii)   the use of fire fighting and other limitation measures; and

    (iii)   the prevention of domino effects;

(c)   the arrangements for alerting individuals on site, neighbouring establishments, where relevant, and the general public to:

    (i)   the hazardous situation;

    (ii)   the nature of the alarms and the plant conditions required to activate them; and

    (iii)   the initial actions required both on site and off site in response to alarms and warnings;

(d)   provisions for establishing and maintaining communications during the emergency response;

(e)   the nature of, and arrangements for maintaining, any mutual aid agreements with nearby establishments, for example provision of equipment and human resources, first aid and specialised medical services;

(f)   the arrangements and conditions for alerting and mobilising:

    (i)   individuals or groups with defined responsibilities under the emergency plans, including essential personnel on site and off site;

    (ii)   the emergency services;

    (iii)   neighbouring establishments, where mutual aid agreements exist; and

    (iv)   off-site agencies;

(g)   the nature and location of any installations which may require special protection, or rescue intervention;

(h)   the nature and location of:

    (i)   emergency control centres - integrity maintained in the event of a major accident or, if not, a reserve facility available;

    (ii)   medical and first-aid centres;

    (iii)   emergency refuges;

    (iv)   sheltering buildings;

    (v)   muster points;

    (vi)   predefined forward-control points; and

    (vii)   any other relevant items;

(i) the location of access routes for emergency services, rescue routes, escape routes, and any restricted areas;

(j) the evacuation arrangements and any transport requirements;

(k) the roll call, and search and rescue arrangements;

(l) the nature and location of any pollution control devices and materials, and the arrangements for subsequent environmental clean up and restoration;

(m) the arrangements for unstaffed or occasionally staffed sites, and sites with staffing levels that vary at different times;

(n) consideration of the effects of emergency response actions, including fire-fighting activities, to minimise the overall impact on people and the environment. This should include short-term and long-term effects, and alternative options for disposal or discharge of released chemicals; and

(o) where relevant, the provision that has been made for monitoring wind speed and direction, and other environmental conditions, in the event of a major accident.

(c) On-site and off-site resources that can be mobilised

461 Your description should relate to the major hazard scenarios described elsewhere in your safety report. You should present enough detail to give those assessing your safety report confidence that the necessary measures have been taken and that the equipment provided is fit for its intended use.

462 Your safety report should describe the on-site and off-site resources which can be mobilised. In this way, you should be able to demonstrate that there are the necessary resources available to contribute to the overall measures necessary to limit the consequences of a major accident to people and to the environment.

463 In providing this information, your safety report should include the resources available:

(a) located on site;

(b) provided by the emergency services;

(c) located at neighbouring establishments with which mutual aid agreements may exist; and

(d) which can be brought in by the operator from elsewhere.

The safety report should also explain how the on-site response will be complementary to, and co-ordinated with, the role of the off-site emergency services.

464 This information should cover the key issues listed here, where appropriate. The following paragraphs provide more detail about the type of information that the competent authority is looking for:

(a) human resources;

(b) hardware fit for purpose when called upon;

(c) personal protective equipment;

(d) fire fighting/fire protection;

(e) minimising the release, and limiting the consequence, of airborne dangerous substances;

(f) minimising consequences of dangerous substances on the ground and in water;

(g) monitoring and sampling;

(h) provisions for restoration and clean up;

(i) first aid/medical treatment; and

(j) ancillary equipment.

Resources that can be mobilised: human resources

465 Your safety report should indicate the personnel that can be made available within

appropriate timescales to carry out the containment actions required by your on-site emergency plan.

466   Your report should show, relating to the conditions on your own site, that:

(a)   the various functions required to implement the on-site emergency response have been identified, and included in the on-site emergency plans and supporting procedures where appropriate, for example operations staff, emergency engineering/repair teams, riggers, drivers, medical staff, special technical experts (such as chemists and toxicologists), fire fighters, and spillage treatment teams;

(b)   the number of people, with the appropriate expertise and training, required to achieve the necessary level of response have been determined, and that these staff can be assembled within the necessary response time;

(c)   the containing actions are achievable in practice, particularly in the early stages of the incident, given the rate at which the accident could escalate; and

(d)   there are contingencies if the 'decision makers' such as operators are incapacitated.

Resources that can be mobilised: hardware fit for purpose when called upon

467   Your safety report should show that you have appropriate arrangements to ensure that equipment is fit for purpose in the event of the major accidents you have identified as reasonably foreseeable.

468   Your report should also describe, wherever relevant, that:

(a)   sufficient quantities of appropriately specified equipment can be made available within the required timescale, and the relevant containing action sustained for the necessary length of time;

(b)   relevant regulations, standards and codes of practice have been followed; demonstration of compliance with these will help the competent authority in accepting your safety report;

(c)   the equipment is capable of operating in the ambient conditions, for example that it has, where necessary, adequate weather protection, including protection from frost;

(d)   the equipment is capable of operating in the conditions expected to be experienced during a major accident;

(e)   emergency equipment is stored in an appropriate manner and location, it is accessible at all relevant times, and it is suitably protected from the consequences of a major accident, for example fire;

(f)   the possibility of losing essential services, such as power, water, communications and other facilities, has been taken into account and alternatives provided where necessary;

(g)   the emergency equipment provided is compatible where necessary with that of the emergency services and that of organisations with which a mutual aid agreement exists, by the provision of adapters where appropriate; and

(h)   electrical equipment used in the emergency response is suitably protected for the foreseeable environmental conditions, so that its use does not introduce additional hazards.

Resources that can be mobilised: personal protective equipment

469   Your safety report should show that suitable and sufficient personal protective equipment (PPE) will be available in the event of a major accident, and that its specifications are appropriate to the range of containing actions required of the response team.

470   There should also be information about whether suitable and sufficient PPE is available for other individuals not directly

involved in dealing with the emergency response, who may be required to wear it, for example emergency escape respirators for site personnel in the event of a toxic gas release.

471   Your description of the PPE provisions should include, where relevant, respirators, breathing air sets, and protective clothing for radiant heat, water, or specific chemical hazards.

Resources that can be mobilised: fire fighting/fire protection

472   If your major accident scenarios include the possibility of fire, your safety report should justify your view that suitable and sufficient on-site fire-fighting and fire protection provisions can be mobilised in the event of a major accident. You should take account of resources available from local and other fire brigades.

473   You should show that the quantity and specifications of the on-site fire-fighting provisions are adequate for the major accident scenarios that you have identified.

474   Where you can foresee circumstances that make the use of fire fighting or other containing measures impracticable or unsafe, for example it may be unsafe to fight certain fires involving explosives, your report should show that your arrangements can identify those circumstances. Also give details of the additional arrangements necessary to limit the consequences of a major accident.

475   The description in your report may include some or all of the following to help make your demonstrations about your ability to limit the consequences of a major accident:

(a)   that the fire-fighting roles of the on-site personnel, for example full-time on-site fire brigade, auxiliary fire fighters, and other site personnel, during an emergency are defined and are appropriate;

(b)   that the fire-fighting roles of the on-site personnel are complementary to the role of the off-site emergency services;

(c)   that the quantity and specification of on-site fire-fighting equipment is sufficient;

(d)   that the water requirements for fire fighting and fire protection, for example cooling, have been predetermined, and that the capacity and reliability of the water supply are adequate, taking into account the various sources which may be available and the time required to establish back-up supplies;

(e)   that suitable and sufficient portable and mobile fire-fighting equipment, such as mobile monitors, mobile pumps, hand/portable extinguishers, foam generation equipment, hoses and hydrants, have been located at appropriate points throughout the installation according to the hazard;

(f)   that suitable and sufficient stocks of foam compound are available when and where necessary;

(g)   that adequate consideration has been given in the design, for example the positioning of walls and fire screens, to assist the positioning and protection of fire-fighting equipment and personnel, and that the reach of fire protection and extinguishing equipment is appropriate; and

(h)   that adequate consideration has been given to flammable substances being carried with firewater and spreading the fire to other areas.

Resources that can be mobilised: minimising the release and limiting the consequences of dangerous airborne substances

476   If your major accident scenarios include the possibility of airborne toxic or flammable substances, your safety report should show that suitable and sufficient provisions can be mobilised to minimise the release of, and limit the consequences of, the substances in the event of a major accident.

477   Your emergency response may include actions to terminate or reduce the leak at

source, such as patching or plugging of leaks in lines and vessels, the closure of valves, and the isolation of sections of plant by blanking off.

478   These actions may be covered by normal operating procedures, but your safety report should still show that you have considered the practicability of carrying them out in the foreseeable accident conditions, and that you have the appropriate equipment, tools and PPE that would be required.

479   Your safety report should also refer to any provisions to reduce the evolution of toxic or flammable fumes from hazardous material that has already been spilt, and to reduce the effects of its fumes.

Example

480   Provisions to reduce fume being given off might include the erection of physical barriers, for example a foam cover, and surface cooling of the spilt material. Measures to reduce the effect of fume might include the use of water sprays to absorb soluble fumes and/or to promote dilution by mixing with air. In such cases, appropriate bunding should also be provided to protect surface and ground waters.

Resources that can be mobilised: minimising the consequences of dangerous substances on the ground and in water

481   If your major accident scenarios include the possibility of dangerous substances being released on the ground or in water, then your safety report should show that suitable and sufficient resources can be mobilised to minimise the consequences of such loss of containment, including in controlled waters. For example, you might refer to your provisions to stop or reduce spillage at source and measures to confine, recover and/or treat the spillage.

482   Your safety report should describe and justify the strategy you intend to adopt in the event of a loss of containment, and show how this is the optimum approach in terms of protecting people and the environment.

483   Confinement of a spillage that could cause a major accident should preferably be achieved by permanently engineered secondary containment systems fitted with an isolation device.

484   The safety report could also identify any resources which may be required, such as:

(a)   earth-moving equipment, sandbags, drain seals, pipeblockers and absorbents for spillages on the ground and in drainage systems; and

(b)   floating booms for immiscible lighter-than-water products that have entered the water, including controlled waters.

485   Your safety report should also describe any provisions for recovering and/or treating spilt material. These provisions might include mobile pumps, and special chemicals and other materials for neutralising or absorbing the spillage. Resources which can be provided by you to assist with the off-site emergency response should also be identified, and there should be confirmation that this information has been made available to the local authority preparing the off-site plans.

Resources that can be mobilised: monitoring and sampling

486   Your safety report should show that you have suitable and sufficient provisions for monitoring and/or sampling which can be mobilised in the event of a major accident.

487   The report should identify the purpose of the sampling/monitoring provision and explain how the results might influence decisions concerning the on-site emergency response.

488   The need for monitoring and/or sampling depends on factors such as the type of hazardous substance involved, the rate at which it might disperse to safe levels, and the speed at which the results can be obtained.

489   Provisions for sampling and monitoring might include the monitoring of oxygen levels, combustible gases and airborne toxic

substances on site and off site, and the taking of samples from air, water and ground. The analysis could be carried out using portable analytical equipment, or static or mobile laboratories.

490   Your safety report should also refer to any special technical expertise and other provisions required to analyse or interpret the results, as well as those sampling and monitoring measures which could help with the off-site emergency response.

Resources that can be mobilised: provisions for restoration and clean up

491   Your safety report should describe the provisions that have been made by you for restoration and clean up of the environment, and which are suitable and sufficient for the major accident scenarios identified in the report.

492   Your safety report could therefore outline what is available for use and who is trained to use it, such as:

(a)   equipment to contain toxic substances;

(b)   agents to soak up and/or neutralise contaminants;

(c)   earth-moving equipment for the removal of contaminated soil and other material;

(d)   booms and skimmers for spillages to water; and

(e)   any temporary storage arrangements, for example portable storage tanks for the contaminated material.

493   Other points to consider include the predicted timescale over which any temporary containment may be required, the arrangements made to ensure that such facilities would not pose an unacceptable threat to health and the environment, and suitable disposal arrangements.

Resources that can be mobilised: first aid and medical treatment

494   Your safety report should show that you have suitable and sufficient provisions to mobilise first aid and medical treatment during the emergency response for the major accident scenarios identified in the report. For medical treatment, it is sufficient to describe the arrangements for transferring employees to hospital as quickly as possible, such as those who have been exposed to toxic substances, if these are your arrangements. In this part of the report, you will need to show how the on-site first-aid provisions dovetail with the provisions in the off-site emergency plan.

Resources that can be mobilised: ancillary equipment

495   Your safety report should show that you have suitable and sufficient provisions to mobilise any ancillary equipment which may be required during the emergency response.

496   Examples of ancillary equipment include vehicles to transport emergency equipment to and from the site of the accident, heavy lifting gear, earth-moving equipment, emergency lighting, and special tools and parts required to carry out emergency repairs and actions.

Maintenance

497   Your safety report should show that you have made suitable arrangements for the maintenance, inspection, examination and testing of your resources and other equipment to be used during the emergency response.

498   The arrangements should cover equipment used for containment, such as fire-fighting equipment, as well as other equipment with a key function, such as alarms to warn personnel of the accident. The information you provide may be confirmation that specific equipment is included in plant maintenance schedules, maintenance records, maintenance procedures and instructions, etc.

Training in emergency response

499   Your safety report should show that you have made suitable arrangements for training individuals on site in the emergency response.

500   The training should cover those members of staff with a specific role in the event of a major accident, as well as providing the training and information for other employees, contractors and visitors to the site. The safety report could also outline the type of information that is provided during such training.

Testing of emergency plans

501   Your safety report should describe the procedures you have, or will be arranging (as and when COMAH requires it (regulation 11 of COMAH[1]), to test and review emergency plans, and to revise the emergency arrangements in the light of lessons learned.

502   Your safety report should describe what arrangements you have drawn up, and what has been implemented to test the emergency arrangements at all levels, for example the local plant response, the site-wide response and the interface with the off-site response.

503   You also need to refer to the arrangements you have for learning the lessons from these exercises, for reviews and for revising the emergency arrangements where necessary.

Summarising the elements that have to be included in the on-site emergency plan

504   Part 2 of Schedule 4, paragraph 5(d) of COMAH requires a summary of the elements discussed in this chapter, that is:

(a)   description of the equipment installed in the plant to limit the consequences of major accidents;

(b)   organisation of the alert and intervention; and

(c)   description of mobilisable resources, internal or external.

505   If you present information about the emergency response in other parts of your report, a summary of the key features of the on-site emergency plan, linked to the relevant and important elements discussed in this chapter, will suffice.

Information required for the off-site emergency plan

506   Your safety report should form part of the supply of information to enable the off-site emergency plan to be drawn up by the local authority. The type of information required by the emergency services is listed in Appendix 2 of HSE guidance HSG191.[2]

507   The minimum information that must be included in your safety report which forms part of this supply of information is listed below (most is considered in more detail in Chapter 3). It is included here as a checklist:

(a)   details of the site, including its location, nearby roads, and site access;

(b)   site plan showing the location of key facilities such as control centres and medical centres, and the location of main process plant and stores;

(c)   details of staffing levels;

(d)   details of the off-site areas likely to be affected by major accidents, and estimates of the levels of harm that might result, for example:

(i)   maps which indicate sectors and environmentally sensitive areas, water abstraction points and sewerage systems should also be noted;

(ii)   information on the types of building;

(iii)   the population density;

(iv)   roads;

(v)   sensitive buildings such as schools and hospitals; and

(vi) a drainage map to help determine where spillages could leave the site;

(e) details of the dangerous substances on site covered by the COMAH Regulations and similar information for other hazardous materials held on site, including:

    (i) quantities;

    (ii) hazardous properties and the nature of their effects on people and the environment;

    (iii) an outline of the use and storage of the materials on site; and

    (iv) an outline of the major accident hazards;

(f) details of the technical advice that your company can provide to assist the emergency response;

(g) relevant technical details of the equipment, and other resources such as fire-fighting chemicals, which may be normally available on site and which may be available to assist the off-site emergency services during an emergency response (also include resources supplied from other establishments with which a mutual aid agreement may exist);

(h) the functions of key posts with duties in the emergency response, their location and how they can be identified, for example:

    (i) the posts authorised to set the emergency procedures in motion and the conditions for doing so;

    (ii) the post responsible for the co-ordination of the on-site containment action;

    (iii) the post responsible for liaising with the off-site emergency services; and

    (iv) the role of any specialist groups required under the on-site emergency plan;

(i) an outline of the initial actions and procedures in the on-site emergency plan, to be taken by on-site staff once the emergency has been declared, for example:

    (i) warning the public and adjacent sites;

    (ii) the setting up of emergency facilities such as the emergency control room; and

    (iii) the response expected from on-site personnel such as sheltering.

Appendices 1 - 4

References

Acronyms and glossary

Appendix 1 Legal overview

	Minimum information required (Schedule 4 Part 2)	For the purpose of (Schedule 4 Part 1)

Chapter 3	Paragraph 2
	
	Presentation of the 'environment' of the establishment including:
	
	(a) description of the site and its environment including the geographical location, meteorological, geographical, hydrographic conditions and, if necessary its history;
	
	(b) identification of installations and other activities of the establishment which could present a major accident hazard;
	
	(c) description of areas where a major accident may occur.
	
	Paragraph 3
	
	(c) description of dangerous substances:
	
	   (i) the inventory of dangerous substances:
	
	      ▲ identification - chemical name, the number allocated by the Chemicals Abstract Service, IUPAC name;
	
	      ▲ maximum quantity present.
	
	   (ii) physical, chemical toxicological characteristics and indication of the hazards both immediate and delayed for both man and the environment;
	
	   (iii) physical and chemical behaviour under normal conditions of use or under foreseeable accidental conditions.
		Provide knowledge and basic understanding to help with each of the demonstrations.
		
		Supply information to enable off-site emergency plan to be drawn up.
		
		Provide sufficient information to the competent authority for providing advice on land use planning as required.

Chapter 4	Paragraph 1 Information on the management system and on the organisation of the establishment with a view to major accident prevention. Description of MAPP and SMS in place (as set out in Schedule 2).	**Demonstrate** that the MAPP, and SMS for implementing the MAPP, have been put into effect.

	Minimum information required (Schedule 4 Part 2)	For the purpose of (Schedule 4 Part 1)
	Paragraph 5 Measures of protection and intervention to limit the consequences of an accident: (b) Organisation of alert and intervention (also see Chapter 7).	
Chapter 5	**Paragraph 3** Description of installation. (a) a description of the main activities and products of the parts of the establishments which are important from the point of view of safety, sources of major accident risks and conditions under which such an accident could happen, together with a description of proposed preventative measures; (b) description of processes, in particular the operating methods. **Paragraph 4** Identification and accidental risks analysis and prevention methods. (a) detailed description of the possible major accident scenarios and their probability or the conditions under which they occur, including a summary of the events which may play a role in triggering each of these scenarios, the causes being internal or external to the installation; (b) assessment of the extent and severity of the consequences of identified major accidents;	**Demonstrate** necessary measures taken to prevent and limit the consequences of major accidents. **Demonstrate** major accident hazards are identified.
Chapter 6	**Paragraph 4** (c) description of technical parameters and equipment used for safety of installations. **Paragraph 5** (a) description of the equipment installed to limit consequences of major accidents (this relates to design features of the installation, supplementing/overlapping the description of the preventative measures).	**Demonstrate** necessary measures taken to prevent and limit the consequences of major accidents. **Demonstrate** adequate safety and reliability incorporated into: (a) design and construction; (b) operation and maintenance. **Demonstrate** that the MAPP, and SMS for implementing the MAPP, have been put into effect.

	Minimum information required (Schedule 4 Part 2)	For the purpose of (Schedule 4 Part 1)
Chapter 7	Paragraph 5 (a) description of equipment installed in the plant to limit the consequences of major accidents (this relates to resources which can be mobilised, rather than design features of the installation, to limit a major accident); (b) organisation of the alert and intervention; (c) description of resources which can be mobilised - internal and external; and (d) summary of information for drawing up on-site plan.	**Demonstrate** necessary measures taken to limit consequences of major accident. **Demonstrate** on-site emergency plans drawn up, and supply information to enable the off-site plan to be drawn up. **Demonstrate** that the MAPP, and SMS for implementing the MAPP, have been put into effect.

Appendix 2 The differences between CIMAH and COMAH safety reports

1   CIMAH reports were submitted to HSE as the competent authority, whereas COMAH reports must be submitted to a new competent authority comprising HSE and the two environment agencies. This reflects the increased importance of providing information about environmental matters and describing the measures for preventing major accidents to the environment, as well as to people.

CIMAH

2   Regulation 7 of CIMAH required the preparation of a safety report to provide information about the dangerous substances, the installation and its surrounding area, the management system, potential major accidents, and a description of the measures to prevent, control or minimise the consequences of any major accident. The information required in a CIMAH safety report was listed in Schedule 6 of the Regulations.

3   The principal objectives of a CIMAH report were stated in guidance (not the Regulations). They were to:

(a)   identify the nature and scale of the use of dangerous substances at the activity;

(b)   identify the type, relative likelihood and consequences of major accidents that might occur; and

(c)   describe the arrangements for the safe operation of the activity, for the control of serious deviations that could lead to a major accident, and for emergency procedures at the site.

4   In other words, CIMAH required information about *what* measures were provided.

COMAH

5   COMAH requires operators to prepare safety reports to demonstrate that all necessary measures have been taken to prevent major accidents and limit their consequences. Safety reports are required to contain information which is sufficient for the purposes of Schedule 4 Part 1, and the minimum information requirements for COMAH reports are listed in Schedule 4 Part 2. In summary, COMAH requires information not only about *what* measures are provided but *why*, for example how they have been arrived at. There is also a two-stage approach for a safety report required for new establishments. At each stage, the competent authority must give its conclusions to the operator.

6   In line with Schedule 4 Part 2, minimum information has to include details about the management system, the environment of the establishment, installations within the establishment, identification and accident risk analysis, and prevention, protection and intervention measures to limit the consequences of an accident.

7   The information provided in a safety report must satisfy the purposes of Schedule 4 Part 1. These purposes include demonstrations that:

(a)   MAPPs, and SMSs for the implementation of MAPPs, have been put into effect in accordance with Schedule 2;

(b)   major accident hazards have been identified, and the necessary measures taken to prevent such accidents and to limit their consequences for people and the environment;

(c)   adequate safety and reliability have been incorporated into design and construction, and operation and maintenance, of any installation, and of any equipment and infrastructure connected with its operation and linked to major accident hazards within the establishment; and

(d)   on-site emergency plan has been prepared.

8   Other purposes of Schedule 4 Part 1 require provision of information to:

(a)   enable the off-site emergency plan to be drawn up; and

(b)   enable the competent authority to provide guidance to planning authorities about the siting of new activities or developments around existing establishments.

9   COMAH specifies the minimum information in a safety report. CIMAH gives absolute information requirements.

10   COMAH has more specific requirements than CIMAH in relation to safety management systems. COMAH has an additional requirement for a written MAPP to cover the overall aims and objectives with respect to control of major accident hazards.

11   There is little difference between CIMAH and COMAH concerning descriptive information about the establishment and installations. Even so, more description is required concerning the environmental surroundings. However, CIMAH related to defined activities in individual installations compared with COMAH, which relates to the whole site. COMAH also requires more detailed information on the characteristics of all dangerous substances on site, not just the scheduled substances.

12   Identification of major accident hazards in COMAH has more emphasis on the environment Apart from this, information requirements about potential major accidents and measures for prevention, control or limitation of consequences are similar for both CIMAH and COMAH reports.

Conclusion

13   The most important change from CIMAH is that, while a CIMAH report provided a description, a COMAH safety report must also fulfil the purposes of safety reports defined in the Regulations. That is, it must make the necessary demonstrations in relation to safe operation of the establishment and present the specified information.

Appendix 3 Dates on which a COMAH safety report is due

Where there is an existing CIMAH report

Date current CIMAH safety report submitted to HSE	Date of update of CIMAH report required (if CIMAH had remained in force)	Date by which a COMAH safety report is required
1 April 1996 to 2 February 1997	Same date between 1 April 1999 and 2 February 2000	3 February 2000 (unless later date agreed by competent authority upon application in writing)
3 February 1997 to 2 February 1998	Same date between 3 February 2000 and 2 February 2001	Same date between 3 February 2000 and 2 February 2001
Dates between 3 February 1998 and 31 March 1999	Same date after 3 February 2001	3 February 2001

1   Some CIMAH reports for larger sites were presented in the form of a core report and separate reports for each installation. The core report dealt with aspects of major hazard control applicable across the whole site. The reports were often submitted at different times, and this has an effect on the due date for the COMAH report.

2   Operators who submitted a core and more than one installation report under CIMAH can choose whether they want to do the same under COMAH, and submit the COMAH report for their establishment in parts. If they do, the due date of the first part will be the date of the first CIMAH report due, but this must be submitted with the information provided in the 'core' report at the same time.

3   For example, a site may have submitted a CIMAH core report on 5 April 1996, and three installation reports: one submitted with the core; a second on 25 December 1997; and another on 31 March 1998. In this case the due date for the first part of the COMAH

report, ie for the core and at least one installation, will be on or before 3 February 2000.

4   In the example above, the COMAH report due on 3 February 2000 can be for the *whole site or just for the core plus one installation,* with the further parts of the COMAH report arriving on 25 December 2000 and on 3 February 2001.

Where no CIMAH report has been required

5   If your site existed on 1 April 1999, but you were not required to submit a CIMAH report, you have until 3 February 2002 to submit your COMAH report.

6   If you have sufficient quantities of dangerous substances to qualify your establishment as a COMAH site, but the quantities are not enough to require a safety report, you will be required to prepare a safety report if the quantities subsequently exceed those in Schedule 1. In these circumstances, you will be required to prepare a report in a

reasonable period of time, which should be discussed with the competent authority.

7   If a dangerous substance, that you are storing or using on your establishment, is reclassified and so you must prepare a safety report for your establishment for the first time under COMAH, then regulation 3(4) allows you 12 months to prepare and submit your report.

Appendix 4 Competent authority view of ALARP

Introduction

1   This appendix outlines some fundamental principles on which the competent authority bases its examination and assessment conclusions on the approaches that you describe in your safety report for hazard identification, consequence assessment, risk analysis and assessment of risks.

2   When the competent authority examines the results of your risk assessment in your safety report, it will be guided by its published approach to risk regulation.[11,12] This is based on the concept of risk tolerability which requires you to:

(a)   take measures to reduce the likelihood of harm occurring from hazards and to limit their consequences until the associated risks are as low as reasonably practicable (ALARP);

(b)   inform those affected about the nature and level of the risks; and

(c)   review risks periodically to see if they can be eliminated or further reduced.

What is hazard?

3   It is often possible to regard any hazard as having more remote causes which themselves represent the 'true hazard'. For example, when considering the risk of explosion from the storage of a flammable substance, it can be argued that it is not the storage per se which is the hazard but the intrinsic properties of the substance stored. Nevertheless, it makes sense to consider the storage as the hazard on which to base any estimation of risk, since this approach will be the most productive one in identifying the practical control measures necessary for managing the risks. Such measures include not storing the substance in the first place, using less of it, or a safer substance, or if there is no alternative to storing the substance, using better means of storing it.

What is foreseeable?

4   The competent authority would not normally expect to consider risks other than those which arise out of reasonably foreseeable events and behaviour. What is reasonably foreseeable depends on the circumstances. For example, the risk of a well-designed, properly built and well-maintained building collapsing would not usually be considered a reasonably foreseeable event (unless signs such as subsidence, cracked walls or falling roof tiles suggest otherwise). This is because the risks were considered and taken care of by the building designers, contractors and maintenance engineers. The building is unlikely to collapse unless there is an external event such as a severe earthquake or explosion, which should be addressed in preparing a safety report. On the other hand, in preparing a safety report you should also consider the effects of an earthquake or explosion more broadly because they could trigger an even greater catastrophic event than the risk of a building collapsing.

What is as low as reasonably practicable (ALARP)?

5   The ALARP concept implies that ultimately there is a trade-off between the costs of risk reduction and the benefits obtained. This concept is sometimes referred to as BATNEEC (best available technology not entailing excessive cost) which is often applied in environmental contexts.

6   Essential considerations for you in achieving risks that are ALARP are:

(a)   the scope you have for hazard elimination; and

(b)   the scope you have for the adoption of inherently safer designs, and the extent to which you have adopted good practice for safe operation. When introducing measures to control risk, the competent authority would expect established good practice to be followed in the first place.

7   If good practice has not yet been established, for example with a novel process, you will have to show that you have implemented risk-reducing measures to the point that the residual risk is ALARP.

8   In the trade-off between the costs of risk reduction and the benefits obtained, there should be a transparent bias on the side of health and safety. Risk reduction measures should be adopted unless the costs, in money, time, and trouble, are grossly disproportionate, or excessive in the case of BATNEEC, compared to the benefits. The extent of the bias depends on the circumstances. In general, the higher the level of risk, the greater the degree of bias that should be shown, and the more the balance should tilt in favour of adopting further measures to reduce the risk. In your report, you therefore need to define the criteria you use for decision making, when demonstrating that all measures necessary for controlling major accident hazards have been taken.

9   Three types of decision making criteria have emerged. The criteria may be used on their own, or in combination with other criteria, depending on the situation. The criteria are:

(a)   Equity-based. These criteria start with the premise that individuals and the environment have a right to a certain level of protection. In practice, this usually results in defining a maximum level of risk or minimum protection standards.

   This approach may be defined in terms of:

   (i)   predetermined levels of safety based on technically achievable standards, for example maximum emission levels (environmental quality standards, EQSs) for particular pollutants; or

   (ii)   risk limits based on historical precedent, for example the maximum tolerable level of the risk of fatality from major hazards for a hypothetical member of the public.[12]

(b)   Utility-based. These criteria apply to the comparison between the incremental benefits of the measures to prevent the risks of injury or detriment, and the cost of the measures. If the level of risk is above a broadly acceptable level, the balance in this cost-benefit approach is skewed towards benefits by allowing a gross disproportion between the costs and the benefits.[12]

(c)   Technology-based. These criteria derive from the idea that a satisfactory level of control is attained when relevant best practice or state of the art technology is employed. Views on good and best practice, and what is state of the art will change as technology advances.

10   In some cases of environmental risk assessment, an equity-based approach to risk regulation is adopted. This approach may be defined in terms of predetermined levels of safety, based on technically achievable standards for particular pollutants, or limits based on historical precedent.

11   The tolerability of risk (TOR) framework[12] brings the equity-based and utility-based approaches together by indicating a 'just tolerable' level above which risk cannot be justified save in extraordinary circumstances. It also applies a lower limit defining broadly acceptable risks below which it is likely that any further risk reduction will be achieved only at grossly disproportionate cost.

12   Residual risks between the two limits need to be ALARP. Most decisions on whether risks are ALARP should be made by exercising professional judgement on whether the risks are reasonable when set subjectively against the cost of further risk reduction. In some cases, a formal cost-benefit analysis can be used which can be seen to give a more objective analysis of costs against the benefits of risk reduction.

13   Some companies have adopted this approach and defined their own ALARP bands. In other cases, more stringent criteria are set for new plant, typically an order of magnitude lower than the band for existing plant.

14   The concept of tolerability implies that existing control measures should be periodically reviewed to ensure they are properly applied and still appropriate. Whether they are still appropriate depends on matters such as:

(a)   the availability of new options for reducing or eliminating risks due to technological progress;

(b)   changes in society's perception of the particular risks;

(c)   changes in our understanding of the risk analysis;

(d)   the uncertainty attached to the risk estimates; and

(e)   new lessons from accidents and incidents.

15   Such reviews should figure prominently in your safety report updates.

16   HSE has as a matter of policy adopted criteria, indicating where the boundaries lie, for risks in a limited category, namely those entailing the risk of death. These criteria are given in the HSE discussion document *Reducing risks, protecting people.*[11] They are guidelines to be interpreted with common sense and are not intended to be rigid benchmarks to be complied with in all circumstances.

References

1   *A guide to the Control of Major Accident Hazards Regulations 1999* L111 HSE Books
     ISBN 0 7176 1604 5 (due to be published August 1999)

2   *Emergency planning for major accidents: Control of Major Accident Hazards Regulations 1999*
     HSG191 HSE Books ISBN 0 7176 1695 9 (due to be published August 1999)

3   Department of the Environment, Transport and the Regions *Guidance on the
     interpretation of a major accident to the environment for the purposes of the COMAH
     Regulations* The Stationery Office 1999 ISBN 0 11 753501 X

4   Environment Agency *Environmental risk assessment as regards COMAH*
     available on the Environment Agency's site on the Internet:
     http://www.open.gov.uk/environment-agency

5   *Major hazard sites and safety reports: what you need to know,* available from the offices of the
     competent authority

6   *Major accident prevention policies for lower-tier COMAH establishments* Chemical Sheet No 3,
     available from the offices of the competent authority

7   *Chemicals (Hazard Information and Packaging for Supply) Regulations 1994*
     SI 1994/3247 HMSO 1994 ISBN 0 11 043877 9 (as amended 1996, 1997, 1998,
     and 1999)

8   *Successful health and safety management* HSG65 HSE Books 1997
     ISBN 0 7176 1276 7

9   BS EN ISO 9001 *Quality management systems*
     available from the British Standards Institution, 389 Chiswick High Road,
     London W4 4AL Tel: 0181 996 9001

10   *Safety advice for bulk chlorine installations* HSG28 HSE Books 1999 ISBN 0 7176 1645 2

11   *Reducing risks, protecting people* discussion document DDE11 HSE Books 1999

12   *The tolerability of risk from nuclear power stations* HSE Books 1992 ISBN 0 11 886368 1

While every effort has been made to ensure the accuracy of the references listed in this
publication, their future availability cannot be guaranteed.

Acronyms and glossary

Acronyms

ALARP	as low as is reasonably practicable
BATNEEC	best available techniques not entailing excessive cost
BLEVE	boiling liquid expanding vapour explosion
CAS	Chemicals Abstract Service
CEPO	chief emergency planning officer
CHIP	Chemicals (Hazard Information and Packaging for Supply) Regulations 1994 as amended by the Chemicals (Hazard Information and Packaging for Supply) (Amendment) Regulations 1996, the Chemicals (Hazard Information and Packaging for Supply) (Amendment) Regulations) 1997, the Chemicals (Hazard Information and Packaging for Supply) (Amendment) Regulations 1998 and the Chemicals (Hazard Information and Packaging for Supply) (Amendment) Regulations 1999
CIA	Chemical Industries Association
CIMAH	Control of Industrial Major Accident Hazards Regulations 1984
COMAH	Control of Major Accident Hazards Regulations 1999
EA	Environment Agency
EQS	environmental quality standard
ETA	event tree analysis
FMEA	failure mode and effects analysis
FTA	fault tree analysis
HAZOP	hazard and operability study
IPC	Integrated Pollution Control
IPPC	Integrated Pollution Prevention and Control Directive
IUPAC	International Union of Pure and Applied Chemistry
LD50	The dose that will kill 50% of the exposed population within a specified period
LPG	liquefied petroleum gas
MAPP	major accident prevention policy
PPE	personal protective equipment
QD	quantity-safety distance
RA	risk assessment
SAC	special areas of conservation
SI	statutory instrument
SMS	safety management system
SPA	special protection areas
SRAM	safety report assessment manual
SSSI	sites of special scientific interest
TOR	tolerability of risk
UN	United Nations
VCE	vapour cloud explosion

Glossary

Assessment

In this context, the process of reading a safety report and reaching a conclusion as to the adequacy of the demonstration that all necessary measures have been taken to prevent major accidents or minimise their effects.

Assessment manager

The field inspector responsible for co-ordinating the various assessment tasks and ensuring that the conclusions are communicated to the operator.

Assessors

The various people who will be completing the assessment process to a plan agreed with the assessment manager. These will include representatives from the various disciplines within HSE and the Environment Agencies.

CAS Number

A unique numbering system used to identify chemicals according to the Chemical Abstracts System scheme.

Competent authority

In relation to an establishment in England and Wales, the Health and Safety Executive and Environment Agency acting jointly. In relationship to an establishment in Scotland, the Health and Safety Executive and Scottish Environment Protection Agency acting jointly (regulation 2(1) refers).

Control system

A means (manual or automatic) for maintaining operating variables within set limits. The primary function of a control system is economic (ie it is intended to ensure that the plant operates efficiently and produces a product that is within specification). If a control system has a role in the defence against excursions outside safety operating limits, then it should be regarded as a safety-related control system.

Criteria

Defined standards of performance against which actual or predicted performance can be assessed.

Dangerous substance

A substance, mixture or preparation:
(a) listed in column 1 of Part 1 of Schedule 1 of the Regulations; or
(b) which satisfies the criteria laid down in Part 3 of Schedule 1 of the Regulations, and present as a raw material, product, by-product or intermediate (regulation 2(1) refers).
Any reference to the presence of dangerous substances should include a reference to the anticipated presence of dangerous substances, and the presence of those which it is reasonable to believe may be generated during loss of control of an industrial chemical process (regulation 2(3) refers).

Demonstration of safety

The process by which the operator provides information and justification to show that all necessary measures to prevent major accidents, or limit their effects, have been taken.

Environment

The surroundings around, over and under an establishment including the flora, fauna, buildings and infrastructure.

Establishment

The whole area under the control of the same person where dangerous substances are present in one or more installation. For this purpose, two or more areas under the control of the same person and separated only by a road, railway, or inland waterway are treated as one whole area (regulation 2(1) refers).

Harm

The severity of the consequences of any potential major accident for people or the environment.

Harm criteria	Essentially dose-response relationships for converting hazardous phenomena (spatial and temporal variations in contamination concentration, overpressure, thermal radiation) into harm for people and the environment.
Hazard	A physical situation with the potential for human injury, damage to property, damage to the environment or some combination of these.
Hazard analysis	The process of identifying undesired events that lead to a hazard being realised, the analysis of the mechanisms by which these undesired events could occur and the estimation of their likelihood and the magnitude of any harmful effects.
Individual risk	The frequency at which an individual may be expected to sustain a given level of harm from the realisation of specified hazards.
Inherent safety	The principle whereby hazards are removed at source by design. Often referred to as the 'inherently safer' approach because in practice, the control of a hazard is achieved at source by design rather than by employing measures to prevent its realisation or reduce the consequences of that realisation after the event.
Initiator (initiating event)	Some event that can escalate and lead to the realisation of a major accident.
Installation	A unit or area in which dangerous substances present are, or are intended to be, produced, used, handled and stored. It includes: (a) equipment, structures, pipework, machinery and tools; (b) railway sidings, docks and unloading quays, serving the installation; and (c) jetties, warehouses or similar structures, whether floating or not, which are necessary for the operation of the installation (regulation 2(1) refers).
Major accident	An occurrence (including in particular a major emission, fire or explosion) resulting from uncontrolled developments in the course of the operation of any establishment, leading to serious danger to human health or the environment, immediate or delayed, inside or outside the establishment and involving one or more dangerous substances (regulation 2(1) refers).
Major accident prevention policy (MAPP)	The operator's policy with respect to the prevention of major accidents.
Management arrangements	In the context of health and safety at work in general, the term applies to an employer's arrangements for health and safety management and covers the elements of 'policy', 'organising', 'planning and implementing', 'measuring performance' and 'audit and review'. The concept is explained in the HSE publication HSG65.[8] In the context of major hazards, the term applies to the operator's arrangements for managing major hazards and covers the same elements but as they relate to the prevention and mitigation of major accidents, ie 'major accident prevention policy', 'organising', etc.
Mitigation	The process of reducing the scale of the consequences of a major accident.
Normal operating limits	The normal operating limits are those operating constraints which apply under all normal operating modes. They are set to ensure that a suitable margin is present between normal operating conditions and the safe operating limits, such as to allow the application of controls (automatic, manual or both) to prevent excursion beyond the safe operating limit. An excursion beyond the normal operating limit will not usually lead to a significantly increased risk of loss of containment, fire or explosion.
Operator	A person who is in control of the operation of the establishment or installation. It is also a person who proposes to control the operation of an establishment or installation which is to be constructed or operated; if that person is not known,

it is the person who in the course of a trade, business or other undertaking carried on by them has commissioned its design or construction. A person may be an individual, corporate body or a partnership (regulation 2(2) refers).

Prevention	The means for eliminating hazards or reducing their likelihood and for mitigating the associated consequences. This includes approaches to inherent safety and identification of suitable control measures.
Process	Any operation by which dangerous substances are handled, or changed in some way. Under CIMAH this was used to determine particular requirements under the legislation, and process was defined by a list of named operations. This is no longer the case in COMAH, which does not distinguish between process and storage.
Protective system	An active or passive means of protecting plant from dangerous conditions either from within (eg overpressure) or without (eg fire).
Qualifying inventory	The quantity of a dangerous substance as defined in Schedule 1 of the Regulations, and used to determine the application of the various provisions of COMAH.
Ramsar sites	These are designated under the Convention of Wetlands of International Importance, especially as waterfowl habitat.
Residual risk	The risk remaining after all proposed control measures for the establishment have been properly implemented.
Risk	The likelihood of a specified undesired event occurring within a specified period or in specified circumstances.
Risk analysis	The process of hazard analysis, and the estimation of associated levels of risk to people, property, the environment or a combination of these.
Risk control system (RCS)	Management system designed to control a particular risk or category of risk. Examples of key RCSs are shown in Figure 2 and discussed at paragraphs 197-200 and 250 onwards.
Risk reduction	The process of risk assessment coupled to a systematic consideration of potential control measures and a judgement on whether they are reasonably practicable to implement. Essentially the process for demonstrating that the adopted controls make the risk to people and the environment ALARP.
Safe operating limits	The safe operating limits are the values beyond which the plant has not been designed to operate safely. They are usually synonymous with plant 'design conditions', ie the conditions against which the plant has been designed, specified and built. An excursion beyond the safe operating limit will result in a significantly increased risk of loss of containment, fire or explosion. Safe operating limits may require to be reviewed periodically, based on the influence of age and condition of the plant and equipment.
Safety critical	In relation to an item, an item of equipment is safety critical if either its failure could cause or contribute substantially to a major accident, or its purpose is to prevent, or limit the effect of, a major accident. In relation to an event, an event is safety critical if its occurrence could lead to a significant release of contaminant with major consequences.
Safety integrity	The probability of a safety-related system satisfactorily performing the required safety functions under the stated conditions within a stated period of time.

Safety management system (SMS)	The concept is explained in the HSE publication HSG65.[8] In the context of major hazards, the term applies to the operator's management arrangements and key risk control systems required for the prevention and mitigation of major accidents, and in scope encompasses the issues described in Schedule 2 of the Regulations.
Safety-related control system	A system which both implements the required safety functions needed to maintain a safe state, and achieves, in conjunction with other risk reduction measures, the necessary safety integrity.
Safety report	A document sent by an operator to the competent authority which is required by regulation 7 of COMAH (Safety reports) or regulation 8 (Review and revision of safety reports).
Site	Where used in this guidance, has the same meaning as 'establishment', which is defined in COMAH.
Worst case scenario	Usually associated with the loss of containment of the maximum inventory of the dangerous substance and the subsequent scenario that produces the worst outcome for people or the environment.

Printed and published by the Health and Safety Executive   C50 7/99